To Christine and Philip

LET'S PLAN A
PARTY

LET'S PLAN A
PARTY

BERNICE WELLS CARLSON

BAKER BOOK HOUSE
Grand Rapids, Michigan

PHOTOLITHOPRINTED BY CUSHING - MALLOY, INC.
ANN ARBOR, MICHIGAN, UNITED STATES OF AMERICA
1978

Contents

*Numbers inside brackets suggest the lowest
age at which the party is usually most enjoyed*

LET'S PLAN A

Let's Give a Party!

*L*ET'S GIVE A PARTY, THE BEST PARTY EVER! WILL IT BE THE biggest party? Oh, no, big parties are often confusing and someone is likely to be neglected.

Will it be the most expensive party? Indeed not! A package of construction paper and a roll of crepe paper can go a long way when cleverly transformed into invitations, decorations, and favors.

Will it be the best planned party? That's the idea. We won't work like beavers making decorations and favors and then say, "Oh, well, the kids will know what they want to play when they get here."

One of three things usually happens at a time like that: no one has any idea what to play; everyone wants to play something different; somebody gets a poor idea involving roughhouse. Then furniture gets broken, the smallest child is hurt, and Mother declares that never again will she give her consent for a party.

We won't let that happen here. We'll plan our party carefully. We'll decide first what activities are suitable in the place where the party is to be given. Running and yelling games are fine in a park, a gym, or even in some recreation rooms, but they are not suitable for living-room parties. Next we'll consider the desires and abilities of each guest. We'll arrange the games so that there is a variety and so that no one will get too tired, and we'll end the affair with good food. Then guests, host, and parents all will say, "That was the best party ever!"

HOW SHALL WE USE THIS BOOK?

All the parties in this book have been carefully worked out. Hundreds of boys and girls have used every idea. Look at the plans thoroughly, decide which might delight your friends most, and then work in your own ideas. After your plans are complete, consult your parents, accept their advice, let them help you where you need help; but keep the party yours.

WHOM SHALL WE INVITE?

Invite children close to your own age. If you are eight and have friends six to ten, why not give two parties—one for your friends under eight and one for your friends over eight? Everyone will understand if you explain that your ten-year-old friends like games where they have to read and write and that your younger friends would feel left out while those games were going on. If you do the work before the party and help clean up when the guests have gone, your mother is likely to prefer two small parties to one large one.

However, if it seems best to have just one party and to invite children of different ages, pick out games that all can play: drawing pictures, pinning the tail on the donkey, making necklaces, finding peanuts. Don't ask a four-year-old to race with a ten-year-old.

If you want to invite three-year-old Tom, who always tags along after his older sister but is too little to play the games you have planned, why not say, "Come in time to eat with us, Tom." Everyone likes to eat with others. If you want to invite twelve-year-old Mary but think she might be bored with games for younger children, why not say as you give her the invitation, "Mary, will you help me with the games at my party? Most of the children are younger than you, but I do want you to come."

WHEN SHALL WE GIVE THE PARTY?

Any time is a good time for a party. Parties need not wait for Halloween, Christmas, or a birthday. In fact, sometimes it is more fun not to have a party right on a birthday. You can have fun with your young friends at your party, and then more fun and surprises at the family celebration on your birthday.

Why not entertain for other people? Introduce the new girl in the neighborhood, say good-by to the boy who is moving away, honor someone's cousins who are visiting in the city. Or give a party just for the fun of it, as your parents do. But whenever you ask people in, be sure to plan ahead what they are to do.

SHALL WE HAVE INVITATIONS?

Invitations are not necessary, but they are fun to make and fun to receive. They are useful, too, because they have the time and place in writing so that no one will get mixed up as to whether you said this Friday or next, 3:30 or 4 o'clock. They can also tell when you would like to have the guests go home.

To make invitations like the ones in this book, place a thin sheet of paper over the picture you want to use and trace it lightly. This is your "master copy" which you use to trace the picture onto your invitations. Although the invitations may be sent out with plain pencil or ink drawings, they are prettier if colored with paints or crayons.

These pictures may help you think of other ideas. You can cut out your tracing of the clown, scout, or cowboy and paste it on construction paper. Or you can make your own free-hand drawings.

If you are helping a younger brother or sister give a party, suggest that he paste on parts of a picture—dots on the clown suit, three balls for the snowman, or parts of the cloth bird.

To make an envelope to hold your invitation, draw a figure shaped like the one on page 14. Be sure that the front and back are the same size, and are a little larger than the invitation. Cut on the straight black lines and fold on the dotted ones. Paste the side flaps to the outside of the back; insert the invitation; then paste down the upper flap.

SHALL WE HAVE DECORATIONS?

Decorations are not really necessary, but they do give atmosphere and help carry out the theme of the party. Be sure to consult your mother as you plan them. No one likes thumbtacks in living-room walls or wood-

Flap

Side Flap

Front

Side Flap

Back

work, but an attic or a game room may be decorated freely. In a living-room, pictures suggesting the party's theme may be mounted on cardboard and placed about the room.

Everyone likes a decorated table. You can use a great deal of ingenuity in designing a centerpiece, favors, and place cards. Start to plan your party some time in advance and spend your spare minutes getting ready for it.

WHAT SHALL WE PLAY AT THE PARTY?

You need not follow any plan in the book exactly. Think of the games your friends like to play, and then, if you like, give the games a new turn to fit in with the theme of your party. For example, you can pin a tail on a donkey, or you can pin the stem on a pumpkin, a hat on a sailor, or a sail on a boat. You can pack your grandfather's trunk; you can also pack Santa's bag, your pirate ship, or your covered wagon.

One new game is enough at a party—especially if the rules are complicated. Have a variety of games and try to give everyone a chance to shine. Have guessing games for "bookish" Peter, running games (if the place permits) for athletic Tom, relay games to promote teamwork, and games that depend on luck.

IN WHAT ORDER SHALL WE PLAY THE GAMES?

Your guests will not all arrive at the same time, so it is well to plan some opening activity that has no special time limit. Why not dress up in old clothes, or make masks, color, work on puzzles, or string beads?

Try to have a quiet game follow an active one. On the other hand, don't ask your guests to sit still too long at one time. Plan some handicraft, singing, or storytelling, just before eating.

Plan more games than you really think you will need. Even the most time-tried games don't always go over with certain groups. If you have an extra game planned you can quickly switch to it. If everyone is happy doing one thing, let them continue longer than you had planned.

That is up to you, but it certainly is not necessary to have a prize for every game. The prizes may be homemade gifts or small purchased ones, like pencils or note pads. One good way to reward the winner is to let him have first choice of a number of favors. Members of a winning relay team·might have first choice of colored lollipops—with enough lollipops for the losers, too.

Don't worry about prizes or favors you have ready for a game you do not play. You can let your guests draw lots for the prize, or open a book and have them guess the number of the page. The person who comes closest gets the prize.

WHAT ABOUT A PARTY FOR MY LITTLE BROTHER?

Watch little children and see how they play. They like to string beads, color, make trains of chairs, march, dance, build garages, put together simple puzzles. Use activities like these in your plans. Some little children like more organized games; for example, pinning the tail on the donkey (without being blindfolded) or "Did you ever see a dolly?" Don't insist that a small child join in a game. He often has a wonderful time watching. There should be no competitive games for little children.

Have you ever noticed that little children seem brightest in the morning? Why not give a party for them then? Have them arrive at 10 o'clock, direct them in their play, serve a simple lunch, and ask the parents to call for them shortly after noon. They are ready then for a nap. This way, the children do not have to wait all day for the party. Morning is not the usual time for a party, but it is a sensible time for preschool or even slightly older children.

Don't make too much of the date of the party, for the sudden appearance of a cold may force you to postpone it. Time doesn't mean too much to little children and "I'm going to give a party some Tuesday morning" is exciting enough.

16

The basic principles are the same for all parties. Consider first the right games for the place where the party is to be given. Then consider the guests. A class or club party could be very much like a party in a home. Even at a church-school-department party or Scout-troop party the same games can be played, although it might be well to divide the guests into small groups. If possible, when giving a large party, divide the guests into approximate age levels, and make sure that a four-year-old is not trying to compete with a ten-year-old. At the end of each chapter in this book is a paragraph telling how to change the plans to allow for a different number of guests.

WHAT SHALL WE EAT AT THE PARTY?

To many girls and boys, party and food mean the same. So serve the food that most people like and which will be sure to agree with them. Let your mother help you plan well-balanced refreshments which are both easy to serve and within a budget.

For a preschool child's party, serve very light food, such as carrot strips, creamed eggs, sponge cake, and ice cream. Give small helpings. Put the milk in small glasses. Little children are more likely to drink it all, and not much will spill if the glass is tipped over. Beware of fruit juices that stain unless there is no tablecloth or rug to worry about.

Why not end a class party with a planned potluck supper, serving perhaps macaroni and cheese, salad, rolls, jello, and cookies?

At an early evening party for young teen-agers, it is all right to serve just ice cream, as the guests have already had dinner.

And after the party is planned? Have fun! You will, at the best party ever!

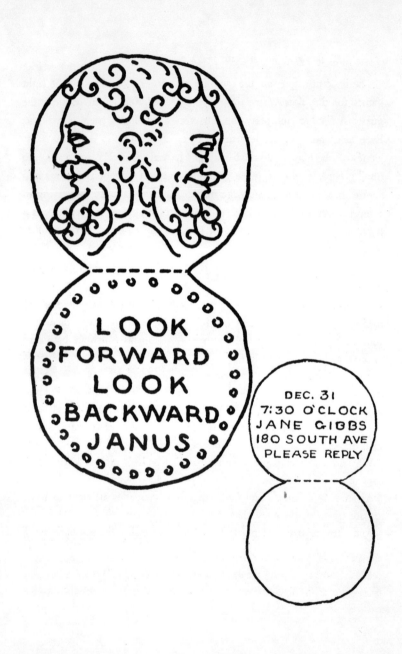

New Year's Party

I'D LIKE TO GIVE A NEW YEAR'S PARTY," SAID TWELVE-YEAR-OLD Jane Gibbs after she heard her elders discussing the approaching holiday.

"That's a splendid idea," answered her mother. "What would you do?"

"What do most people do on New Year's Day?—That's an idea, Mother; I'll find out what most people do—people everywhere—and I'll use their celebrations in my party plans."

Jane quickly donned her bright red parka and slipped into her woolly jacket, fastening the last button as she closed the door of her home on the way to the library. There she found all kinds of interesting information about various celebrations and tabulated them.

"How can I use all these notes?" she asked herself. Suddenly she had a bright idea—a scavenger hunt, one which would start early in the evening before all the adults were on the streets en route to their various parties. She decided to put objects on the list that were symbolic of New Year's celebrations in other lands. A few of her findings she saved as ideas for games after the hunt.

Her first concrete problem after solving that of the general idea was that of making invitations. She learned that Janus was the old Roman god of the New Year and that his motto was, "Look forward, look backward."

"Still very good advice for the New Year," Jane thought.

She made a trial invitation on the fold of a sheet of paper and cut it to represent an old Roman coin with a picture of the two-faced god on its surface. On the inside she wrote the particulars of the invitation, and on the back she wrote Janus' slogan. She found she could make quite a realistic coin by painting the entire sheet with soft yellow water colors and drawing over the first lines of the face with India ink. Suddenly a better idea came to her. She remembered seeing some silver construction paper that would take India ink in a stationery store. Her invitations made from this looked like huge ancient silver coins.

When all the guests were present, Jane explained her idea for the scavenger hunt and revealed why she had chosen each object on her list.

"In many countries New Year's Day has been set aside for calling," she said; "so the first thing on the list is a calling card. In old Persia, friends brought each other eggs; so an egg must be obtained, unbroken. The Scotch children are known to beg for oatmeal cookies on this day; so you might find one of those. In days of old, English nobles took this time especially to bring gifts of jewelry to their sovereign; so there is a necklace on the list.

"The Chinese really make an occasion of the event and celebrate for three days, decorating their homes with red paper. You must find a piece. The Belgian children, so the story goes, try to confiscate all the keys in their homes and lock aunts and uncles in a room. The unsuspecting relatives must pay forfeits before they can be released. You must get a key. The last object is in honor of the Roman god of the New Year, Janus. You must get his picture."

She divided the guests into groups of equal numbers and asked each group to select an umpire. She gave each leader a pencil, a paper sack in which to collect the loot, and a list which read: "calling card, egg, oatmeal cookie, necklace, red paper, key, picture of Janus."

Her rules were very simple: an adult was asked to go with each group; the teammates had to stay together; every object on the list had to be obtained in the order in which it was requested; no two objects were to be obtained from the same home; the place of the finding had to be recorded; and all had to come back by nine o'clock whether they had completed the list or not.

Off the gangs started, stopping only for a minute to confer upon the closest and most likely place to find a calling card. One little girl knew the people who lived next door to Jane's family; so her group went in a body to the house, and the little girl rang the bell.

"Good evening," she said, as her friend opened the door. "We are having a scavenger hunt, and on our list is a calling card. May we have one of yours?"

The friend gladly gave a card, and all called, "Happy New Year!" as the gang went on its way. Many groups stopped at homes of their teammates who knew they had certain objects needed. Friends and families were glad to see the happy youngsters and to give them what they requested if they could. Oatmeal cookies were the hardest objects to find, and each group made several stops before they had their loot.

One team was very lucky. The mother of the leader had baked oatmeal cookies that very morning, and they finished long before the other children. Jane set up tables, and they had a good time among themselves playing checkers, dominoes, and other quiet games until the others returned.

The first big job was examining everybody's loot. Sure enough, everyone had everything that was needed. Jane gave each member of the team which had first returned a lucky penny of the closing year.

HUT AB

Jane next told her friends about an old German custom. "Tradition says," she explained, "that boys used to shout 'Hut ab' when on New Year's Eve they saw a man wearing a silk topper after dark. If he did not remove it at once, it was their privilege to knock it off and destroy it."

Down to the basement the friends went, where Jane had a big black hat made from a tin can with a heavy construction-paper brim balanced on a football, which was set in another can. The guests roared when they saw the funny-looking fellow, and began to call, "Hut ab."

Jane asked the guests to line up, and in turn each threw a rubber ball at the hat. Each person who hit it received a point of one, and each person who knocked it over received five. Everyone was given a paper hat to wear when the game was over.

21

NEWSPAPER RACE

"So much happened last year," Jane told her friends, "that it was rather hard to keep up with our daily newspapers. We'll see what we can do now."

She divided the guests into relay teams and gave each leader two newspapers. The object of the race was for the contestant to lay one paper on the floor and put one foot on that, place the other paper ahead of it and put his other foot on that, progress across the room in this manner, return in like manner, and give the papers to the next person in line to do likewise. As she gave the signal, the leaders started out. They certainly looked funny stretching their legs and trying to balance as they laid down papers. One boy reached too far and fell over, and had to go back and start again. Each person had a chance to race; but the team which finished first, of course, was pronounced the winner. The game was repeated several times.

REFRESHMENTS

Some of the guests had had trouble early in the evening finding oatmeal cookies. There was no trouble at the close of the party, for Jane passed around dozens of them and hot steaming chocolate.

"There is an old American custom I almost forgot," said Jane, "that of blowing horns on New Year's Eve."

She passed out all manner of noise makers and then suddenly stopped the racket to remind her friends that, being good Americans, they just couldn't end a New Year's party without singing "Auld Lang Syne."

The party broke up early, many parents calling for their youngsters. Jane's father saw to it that none of the children wandered around the street late at night.

SUGGESTIONS

Children from eight to fourteen years of age will enjoy this party. Children under twelve years of age should give it during the afternoon. Church and school groups will find the party one solution for what to let

22

children do on New Year's Eve that they will enjoy, a party suited to their own age group. It may be given for a group from six to any number of children.

A sturdy black hat may be made by painting a gallon fruit juice can and supplying a rim of heavy construction paper, cardboard, or plywood. If, however, it is desirable to have all the games in the living room, a hat may be made of construction paper or light cardboard, and the guests may throw ping-pong balls at it.

If there is more time after all the games have been played, the boys and girls may write down all the events of importance which happened during the closing year. The person who remembers the most receives a prize of a new calendar.

The guests may see who had the most lucky days in the closing year, by playing the ring toss game in the Skipper Party (page 94).

MATERIALS NEEDED

Invitations: Paper, water colors, India ink.

Games: Paper bags, pencils, lists of objects to be obtained on hunt, set games, black hat, balls, newspapers, paper hats, noise makers.

PLEASE COME
TO MY
SNOW PARTY
SATURDAY
4 O'CLOCK
RICHARD BARRY
184 SHERMAN AVE
PLEASE REPLY

Snow Party

$\mathcal{A}$S THE COLD NORTH WIND BLEW WITH GREAT GUSTO, WHISKING fallen snow into little piles around the house, Richard Barry and his mother sat before the cozy fireplace in their big living room making paper snowmen to carry invitations to a snow party. Although Richard was only five years old, he was able to draw simple figures of snowmen with charcoal eyes and mouths and carrot noses. He made sure that each man had at least one arm showing. His mother wrote the particulars of the invitation on a small sheet of paper, rolled it up like a scroll, cut little slits on either side of the arm, and slipped in the note. Richard put the invitations into the envelopes and later did the mailing himself.

On another stormy afternoon, Richard made many, many paper snowflakes to look like the real tiny flakes which his mother showed him under a magnifying glass. His mother made an equilateral triangle of cardboard and showed him how to fold a square of thin white paper in half, place a point of the triangle in the center of the crease with the edge along the crease and fold the rest of the paper over the cardboard form twice so that the sheet was folded into sixths—for all snowflakes are six pointed. Then she showed him how to fold again in the center of the angle (to make the points symmetrical), tear along the outer edge in uneven fashion, and tear little pieces out of the folded edges. When he opened up his sheet, there was a lacy pattern, just like a huge snowflake. He made dozens of these; and on the afternoon of the party, he placed them all about the living room.

SHOVELING SNOW

As each tot arrived, he was given a tiny pail. When all were present, Richard explained that he would like them to pick up all the snow they

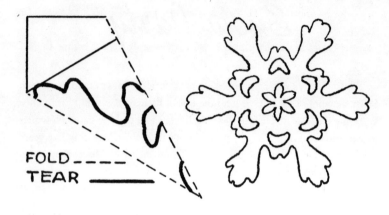

FOLD _____
TEAR _____

could and put it into their containers. Of course the snow was easy to find, but there were no two flakes on top of each other. After they had all "shoveled" for five minutes, Richard's mother assured them that she was certain that they had all the needed snow and told them that each might keep his pail and flakes. To make sure that there would be no confusion when the tots were ready to take their playthings home, she wrote the name of each guest on the bottom of his pail and asked him to put it with his snow suit.

JACK FROST AND THE FLOWERS

Richard's mother gathered the children around her and asked them if they knew what happened to the little flowers before the first snow fell in the winter. One little boy answered that Jack Frost nipped them and they were frozen. Richard's mother agreed that that might happen and explained how a careful gardener would want to cover up his plants and let them go to sleep before the roguish Jack Frost arrived. She chose one little boy to be Jack Frost and a little girl to be the very careful gardener, Mistress Mary. All the other children were flowers. After Richard's mother had explained the game, all the little flowers lined up on one side of the room with Mistress Mary standing near them. Jack Frost stood in front of them.

Mistress Mary began the game by saying, "Come, flowers, it is time to go to bed."

They answered, "We are not afraid of Jack Frost."

"You will be sorry," said she. At that signal the little flowers tried to run across the room to a spot marked as their safety goal, but Jack Frost nipped (tagged) two of them before they were safe. These two also became Jack Frosts. In just a few minutes the last little flower was tagged, and he became the first Jack Frost as the game was repeated.

SNOW BATTLE

A snow battle was next on the program. The guests were divided into two groups and stood on opposite sides of the room behind two imaginary lines. Each child was given five paper snowballs (sheets of paper crushed together). At a signal, everyone tried to throw his balls across the opponents' line. Whenever a ball fell short, the thrower ran out, returned to his line, and threw again. As a ball crossed a line, the opponent picked it up just as quickly as he could and tossed it back. The air was full of paper snowballs; but no one minded getting hit, as it didn't hurt in the least. After ten minutes of the battle, Richard blew a whistle to stop the game. The balls were counted and the team with the fewest on its side won.

SNOWBALL TOSS

Richard and his friends collected all the balls, and his mother divided them again. She asked the tots to sit in a circle; and when they had done so, she placed a big hat in their midst. In turn each child threw a snowball. Some went in the hat and some did not. When one failed to go in, the thrower took it back. The game moved very quickly, each child tossing just as soon as the one sitting next to him had finished. At last one little boy had all his balls in the hat, and the game ended.

Jack Frost is famous as an artist of color, and Richard knew that there are no daintier hues anywhere than those found in soap bubbles. He asked his friends to come up to his bedroom, where he easily picked up the rugs. As he gave each guest a clay pipe, the inside of which was painted with water colors, his mother brought in a big pan of soapsuds containing two tablespoons of glycerine to a pint of water. The children sat on the floor and blew their bubbles. Then they tried to see who could blow the longest chain, and who could blow the biggest single bubbles. Richard's mother showed them how to bounce them. Since Richard's daddy was home from work by this time, he and mother held a blanket taut as Richard blew a bubble and lightly dropped it. His parents shook the blanket gently and the bubble rolled from end to end. How the little boys and girls shouted with glee as they watched the bubbles roll about!

The blowing only stopped when the children heard the sound of music, which Richard explained was Jack Frost's summons to supper downstairs. The children tucked their pipes away with their little pails. The dishpans were all carefully picked up before the children left the room.

REFRESHMENTS

The table was covered with a white crepe-paper spread with icicles cut in its sides. Popcorn balls with funny little pipestem-cleaner men astride them marked each place, and a cake with white frosting formed the centerpiece.

At this white (or almost all white) banquet, Richard served rolled jelly white-bread sandwiches, creamed eggs, milk, ice cream, and the cake.

SUGGESTIONS

Children from four to seven years of age will enjoy this party, which may be given in a living room or recreation room of a home. It might be well to limit the number of guests to about eight, so that the children will not become too excited. The plans, however, will work for a larger number if the space where the party is given is adequate. School and church groups can use these plans by substituting "winter sports" for the bubble-blowing, which might prove rather messy with too many children doing it. The children could make the invitations and the snowflakes in class.

Far less perfect snowflakes with only four points may be made by young children who are unable to grasp the idea of using the triangle to make the six-pointed snowflake. To make these, fold a sheet of paper in quarters and tear as directed in the plans.

WINTER SPORTS

If the host thinks there is too much running with the Jack Frost game, or the bubble blowing is not feasible, a "winter sports" game may be played.

All but one of the children are seated on chairs in a circle. Each child is given the name of some sport, such as skating, sliding, skiing. The lone child starts the game by saying, for instance, "Today I should like to build a snowhouse and have a snowball fight." The children named "Build a snowhouse" and "Have a snowball fight" change places as quickly as they can as the child in the center tries to slip into one of their chairs. If he succeeds, the child left standing repeats the game, giving the names of two other sports. If the change is made before the child in the center sits down, he tries his luck again. After two unsuccessful tries, he chooses a successor.

If there is time after all the games have been played, the guests might tear snowflakes.

MATERIALS NEEDED

Invitations: Paper, pencil, crayons, scissors.

Decorations: White crepe-paper tablecloth with icicles on edges, popcorn balls, pipestem-cleaner men.

Games: Paper snowflakes, tin pail for each guest, five paper snowballs for each guest, hat, whistle, clay pipe with bowl painted with water color for each guest, soap bubble water with two tablespoonsful of glycerine added for each pint of water, blanket.

Valentine Party

As the fourteenth of February drew near, Phyllis Harper was very, very busy making valentines. At first glance they appeared to be just ordinary greetings, but upon closer inspection they proved to be invitations to a party. Phyllis folded a sheet of paper and traced the picture of an old-fashioned girl on the outside, colored it, and pasted parts of a lacy doily around the edges. On the inside she wrote her message.

After her invitations were in the mail, she busied herself with the decorations. She cut dozens and dozens of red hearts of construction paper, strung them together with red twine, and hung them from the archways and around the windows of the living room of her home.

Then Phyllis decided it would be fun to make lollipop dolls as favors for the table. She cut a strip of crepe paper about ten inches long and as wide as the length of a lollipop, pasted its sides together, slipped it over the lollipop stick, and wound a pipestem cleaner around just below the candy with ends extended like arms. She turned down the paper which covered the candy (making a ruffle), fluffed the skirt, pasted a paper face on the wrapped candy, and placed the stick in a gumdrop base.

"Are your boys going to wear skirts too? Or aren't you going to have boys?" asked her Uncle Henry, who had put down his paper to watch her complete a doll with a sea-green skirt.

"I suppose the boys would prefer boy dolls," answered Phyllis. "Maybe I can make a lollipop doll with trousers."

She soon designed a doll with a pipestem cleaner for one leg and the stick for the other, covering these with trousers made of strips of crepe paper pasted into tubes. The blouse was like the lady's frock, but short; and the pipestem cleaner arms also held the long trouser legs in place. With gumdrop shoes the boy was able to stand alone. Phyllis felt certain her friends would have no objections to the dolls' big feet as long as they were made of candy.

POSTMAN

The first game at her party was truly a mixer and honored the man who for decades has been Cupid's messenger, the postman. Phyllis asked her guests to sit on chairs placed in a circle and gave each one the name of some city. She stood in the middle of the circle and said, "I have a letter to be sent from Boston to New York." Just as she had directed, the two children named Boston and New York tried to change chairs as Phyllis quickly slipped into New York's place, leaving Boston without a seat. Phyllis took the name Chicago, and Boston called for Milwaukee and Lansing to change. As they happened to be sitting next to each other, Boston was again without a chair and called for Denver and Los Angeles. This time Denver was left alone. The game moved quickly; and as soon as everyone had several chances to change chairs, Phyllis asked her guests what they could get out of "Valentine Greetings."

VALENTINE GREETINGS

The young people looked very puzzled until Phyllis explained the meaning of her queer question. She passed out pencils and slips of paper with the letters V A L E N T I N E G R E E T I N G S across the top, telling them to make all the words they could using these letters, such as "net" and "green." Phyllis ruled that no letter could be used more times than it appeared in the two words, no proper names would count, and that all words had to be spelled correctly to score. The children felt very smart as they started to write down the words. There were so many that they could see at first glance, words that even the worst speller could recognize at once. Phyllis let the guests write for fifteen minutes and then collected the papers, as the children asked each other, "How many did you get?" Phyllis' mother offered to correct the papers as all joined in musical hearts.

MUSICAL HEARTS

The game was played just like "going to Jerusalem" except that construction paper hearts, six inches across the largest part, were used in the place of chairs. There was one less heart than the number of guests. Phyllis placed them in two vertical lines; and, as music was played, the guests marched round and round. Suddenly the music stopped; each guest stooped to pick up a heart; and the person left empty-handed withdrew from the game, taking a heart with him. He had a lot of fun watching the others, for there was such a mad scramble, and after each game he had another friend on the sidelines. Soon there were only two guests left playing. Phyllis decided to stop the game there and give each one a candy heart award, for she feared that they might bump their heads reaching over to pick up the remaining heart.

HEART TOSS

The sight of candy made everyone's mouth water more than a little bit; so Phyllis gave each guest a dozen tiny candy hearts with the instructions that they could eat three apiece. Eating more, she said, would spoil their chances in the candy toss. According to Phyllis' directions the guests lined up back of the border of the rug. Phyllis placed a candy box in the center of the room. In turn each guest approached a certain spot, tossed three candies, and went to the end of the line as Phyllis kept account of his score. The rounds were made three times and the scores were added up. One little boy actually put eight hearts into the box, and Phyllis assured him that he really deserved the bag of hearts which she gave him.

Phyllis' mother entered the room just as the guests were congratulating the champion tosser, and announced the winner of the spelling game, a little girl to whom she gave a box of "ready-to-make" valentines.

MAKING VALENTINES

The guests gathered around the winner, and some even remarked that they thought she was mighty lucky to win a prize like that. It provided a

golden opportunity for Phyllis to suggest that all the guests might make valentines. She spread newspapers over the floor and brought out scissors, construction paper, paste, lace doilies, valentine stickers, pencils, and crayons. During the remaining part of the afternoon, the boys and girls busied themselves with making really lovely greetings. Phyllis assured them that they could take home all they made to send to their other friends. One little boy was quiet for some time and spoke at last.

"You know, Phyllis," he said. "I have all my valentines. If you don't mind, do you know what I would like to do? I wish I could take mine to the children at the orphanage. I bet they won't get very many, and perhaps some of the little tots would like to have some early to give to other boys and girls of their same age—you know, sort of surprise each other on Valentine's Day."

"I like that idea," said a little girl. "I am going to do the same thing."

"So am I! So am I!" the others chirped.

"I have an idea," said Phyllis' mother. "Suppose you each make a big envelope, write your name on the outside, and I'll take them down in a group. Better still, each of you could leave yours there on your way home, but I'll call the orphanage so that the matron will expect you."

NOBLE AWARDS

"You are all so noble," said Phyllis. "I think you should be decorated." She took down the strings of hearts from the decorations and draped one over each of the girls' shoulders. Without any suggestion from the hostess, the guests started to pick up all the papers, even the tiny scraps. Soon the room was spick and span.

MATCHING HEARTS

"Broken hearts are sad things, but many are mended on St. Valentine's Day," said Phyllis, as she gave each guest half of a construction paper heart. The boys and girls soon noticed that the edges were rough where the heart had been cut in two, so Phyllis told them that they would find partners for the grand march to supper if they would match notches. As Phyllis' mother played familiar love songs, the guests marched round and round the living room and finally into the dining room.

REFRESHMENTS

The table was centered with a big cake with the outline of a heart made in its center. From it radiated rows of tiny candy hearts. A lollipop doll marked each place.

Strawberry gelatine fruit salad, heart-shaped sandwiches covered with cream cheese to which cherry juice had been added, and the cake formed the menu.

SUGGESTIONS

Boys and girls from ten to fourteen years of age will enjoy this party. If it is given in a home, the number of guests should be limited to about twelve. Church and school groups may give it for large numbers with very little change, merely dividing the guests into small groups for various contests.

CANDY GUESSING

If there is time after all the other games have been played, the guests will enjoy trying to guess the number of candy hearts in a glass jar.

Guests may also enjoy dropping candy hearts into a bottle while looking in a mirror as in the Humpty Dumpty Turned-Around Party (page 57).

MATERIALS NEEDED

Invitations: Paper, pencil, lace doilies, crayons or paints, and paste.

Decorations: Construction paper hearts strung on red twine, paper and colors for lollipop faces, lollipops, crepe paper, gumdrops, pipestem cleaners.

Games: Chairs for all, pencils, paper for each guest with letters V A L- E N T I N E G R E E T I N G S written across top, construction paper hearts six inches across widest part for all but one guest, music, candy box, twelve candy hearts for each guest, materials for making valentines, hearts cut in two with ragged edges.

Favors: Two candy hearts, bag of candy hearts, ready-to-make valentines.

PLEASE
COME TO MY
GEORGE
WASHINGTON
PARTY, SAT.
FEB. 22, 3 O'CLOCK
BILL ADAMS
318 PINE ST.
PLEASE
REPLY

George Washington's Birthday Party

*Y*ANKEE DOODLE MAY HAVE BEEN A DANDY, BUT THE PAPER Colonial gentlemen which Bill Adams sent to bear invitations to his George Washington party wore warm wool caps and mufflers reminiscent of the days of Valley Forge. Bill made his figures so that the top of each messenger's hat fell on a fold and inside wrote the time and place.

To give his home a patriotic atmosphere, Bill borrowed flags and bunting from several of his friends and placed them about the living room. He cut a picture of Washington from a magazine, mounted it on cardboard, and hung it above the mantel.

TRACK MEET

When all the guests were present, Bill reminded them that the "father of our country" was not only "first in war, first in peace, and first in the hearts of his countrymen," but also first in nearly every athletic event in which he participated. The guests were asked to draw from a box little figures, some hatchets and some cherries. By matching their tokens, the boys and girls formed teams and upon Bill's request chose contestants for the following events: the broad jump, the high hurdles, the high jump, and the tug of war. Bill explained that scores would be given as in a track meet: five for first place, three for second, two for third, and one for fourth.

BROAD JUMP

Of course, the teams selected their longest legged members for the broad jump, only to learn to their dismay that Bill wanted them to smile. Tape

37

measure in hand, he measured the width of each contestant's broadest grin and scored the teams.

HIGH HURDLES

Another set of youngsters who lined up for the high hurdles soon learned that their obstacles were ordinary soda crackers. Following Bill's instructions, they ate them as quickly as they could and whistled.

HIGH JUMP

Little did the high jumpers guess what was in store for them. In turn Bill asked each guest to sing as high as he could. Those who reached a fairly high note competed against each other. One by one the singers were eliminated until there were only two little girls competing. Bill just could not decide which one was singing the higher tone, so he let them score five points apiece, gave the third person two and the fourth one.

TUG OF WAR

Everyone took part in the tug of war. Each member of the cherry team was paired off with a member of the hatchet team. Each couple was given a long string with a red candy cherry tied equidistant from its ends. Bill set up a few rules: at his signal, each guest had to put the end of his string in his mouth and place his hands behind his back; at another signal, they were to start to chew toward the cherry; anyone who jerked or pulled was out of the game; and anyone who dropped his string had to start again from the beginning. The guests started to chew and chew. A few of them dropped their strings because they just could not help laughing. Each one to reach the center before his opponent scored five for his team.

It took Bill little more than two minutes to add up the team scores, which showed the cherry team had won. He gave each member a candy cherry.

BOSTON TEA PARTY

"One of the big events of the Revolution was the Boston tea party," Bill reminded his guests. "Now we'll see how good you can be at keeping the tea away from old John Bull." He asked one boy to be John Bull and directed the other guests to sit in a circle around him. He gave a tea bag to one of the girls in the circle, a patriot, and requested her to toss it across the circle to another American while John Bull endeavored to catch it. Back and forth it went very quickly until at last the Englishman intercepted it. The man who made the unfortunate toss, became the Englishman in the center of the ring. Faster and faster the bag flew through the air, and more and more frequently the guests changed places, until at last Bill called a halt to the game, saying he wanted some first-class spies to carry messages.

SPY RELAY

The cherry and the hatchet teams lined up behind their captains ready to carry important papers. Bill gave each leader five small sheets of tissue paper, asked him to balance them on his curved arm, and at a signal to carry them across the room, return with them to his team, and give them to the next in line who would do the same thing. The leaders started off. Some walked too rapidly so that the papers blew off and they wasted time picking them up. Those who walked cautiously were the first to return to their teams. Each guest had an opportunity to carry papers for his country; but the hatchet team finished first and the members were given cloth badges to pin to their garments as symbols of honor.

HISTORIC PANTOMIME

"I've been telling you what to do, more or less," said Bill. "Now I'll let you use some of your own ideas. Suppose you act out some early American stories. Oh, they don't have to be long ones, just little short skits that we can all guess, like Paul Revere's ride. I'll divide you into groups of three people and you may choose props from anything in this box. There is only one rule: everybody must do something."

There was a great humming and tittering as the groups got together and began to make their plans. Then boys and girls started to maul through the scarfs, drapes, tub, flags, and old clothes which Bill had placed in the box to which he had pointed as he spoke. Two boys began to argue about an old coat, until suddenly they realized that whoever was called upon for his stunt first could use it then give it to his friend to use. Bill gave his guests just ten minutes to get ready and then called, "Curtain." He requested all his actors to be seated on the floor and then stood before them.

"Ladies and gentlemen," he said. "As a fitting climax to this patriotic party, I have called upon some of the best actors in America to re-enact for you some of the events of our early history. These actors have slaved night and day to prepare the skits for you. Please let no one speak until they have finished each act. If you cannot guess the story which they are re-telling, remember that the fault may lie in your lack of knowledge of the history of our country, not with their acting. The first scene from the distant past will be presented by Phil Byrd and his players."

The three actors tied scarfs over their heads, huddled close together blowing on their hands and stamping their feet, and murmured half sentences about the cold and fires back home.

"Washington at Valley Forge," the children called.

The next group climbed into the tub as two of them pretended to row and the third stood with arms crossed as if in front of the boat.

"Washington crossing the Delaware," the children easily guessed.

The scene of the Boston tea party and the "Spirit of '76" were also enacted. By popular request another ten minutes were given the guests, and each group acted out another story.

REFRESHMENTS

The program was halted by the sound of a bugle blowing mess call. As Bill's mother played a familiar minuet, the guests walked two by two into the dining room. A little artificial tree with candy cherries tied to its branches centered the table, and at the places were rubber hatchets for the boys and inexpensive dolls in crepe paper Colonial dress for the girls.

Although the soldiers at Valley Forge were glad to see almost any food, these young patriotic guests of Bills were particularly pleased to see a

Mount Vernon dinner of baked ham, sweet potatoes, corn, biscuits, and cherry tarts.

SUGGESTIONS

This party is planned for boys and girls from the ages of eight years to fourteen. As there is no running, it may be given in almost any kind of room. As few as ten or twelve guests may take part, or it may be given for large school or church classes. Of course, simple refreshments may be substituted for the dinner if there are many guests. Cherry ice cream and wafers may well be served.

CROSSING THE DELAWARE

If there is time, the guests may enjoy a "crossing-the-Delaware" relay. The guests are lined up with teams behind each captain. A bowl of ice cubes is placed before each leader, and he is given a spoon. He must balance as much ice as he can get on the spoon without using his hands, carry it across the room to another bowl, deposit it, and return to his team, giving the spoon to the next person in line, who repeats the action. Each person present has a chance to compete. There are two prizes, or awards of honor, given: one to team members who finish first, and one to team members having the most ice in the opposite bowl.

MATERIALS NEEDED

Invitations: Paper and coloring equipment.

Decorations: Flags, bunting, picture of Washington mounted on cardboard, artificial tree with cherries attached.

Games: Paper hatchets and cherries by which teams may be selected, tape measure, soda crackers, strings with candy cherries tied equidistant from the ends, tea bag, slips of tissue paper, costume and prop materials.

Favors: Candy cherries, badges made by pasting patriotic stickers on cloth, rubber hatchets, Colonial dolls.

41

St. Patrick's Day Party

*P*ATTY O'CONNOR'S IRISH EYES WERE REALLY SHINING AS SHE thought of plans for her St. Patrick's Day party. Weeks before the scheduled day she started to make her invitations, paper men of Erin with notes in their back pockets. To make each one, she folded a sheet of paper in half, traced the outline of the man, cut it out, drew his features on the front half and his hands and clothing both back and front, colored them, made a slit at the top of the back pocket, and pasted the sides of the figure together. She wrote the particulars of the invitation on a piece of paper two inches by one inch, folded it, and inserted it in the slit.

After her invitations were in the mail, Patty set about to make dozens of shamrocks of construction paper for decorations and to use in games. On the back of some she wrote crazy fortunes. She pinned these to the curtains and stuck others in the frames of pictures.

HOT POTATO

"Of course all good Irishmen like potatoes, but no one wants to hold a hot one too long," Patty reminded her guests, when all had arrived. She asked the boys and girls to sit in a circle and produced a potato which she called "hot." Her mother started to play some old Irish tunes as Patty explained the game. The object was to toss the potato around the circle, passing it from person to person. Anyone who dropped it was out of the game, and anyone holding it when the music stopped was out. How quickly the potato moved as the music started up! Of course being caught with it when the music stopped was just everyday bad luck for one boy; but he took his lot cheerfully and withdrew from the circle. He soon had company, for Patty's mother never played very long at a time and never stopped at the same place when she repeated a piece. Soon there were only two guests competing. One of them dropped the potato, so the other was pronounced the winner and given a musical sweet potato on which to play.

KISSING THE BLARNEY STONE

"If you ever go to Ireland, you'll want to kiss the Blarney stone," said Patty. "But don't you think you should have a little practice first?" She asked the guests to form a circle and then placed a smooth white stone in their midst. In turn each guest was blindfolded, requested to place his hands behind his back, turned around three times, and told to walk to the place where he thought the stone might be, kneel down, and touch his head to the floor. Each time a guest touched his head to the floor, Patty marked the spot with a shamrock. Some of the guests were very near the stone, others several feet away; but one little boy almost touched the spot. He was given a book of Irish jokes.

PIG IN THE PARLOR

"They kept the pig in the parlor, for he was Irish too," hummed Patty as she picked up the shamrocks from the floor. "Don't you know that old song?"

She sang it for them and then suggested that they all join in playing "pig in the parlor." She chose one child to be the health inspector who did not approve of pigs in the home, and asked the other guests, all Irishmen who did not want to give up their family pets, to sit in a circle around the inspector. The pig was a small ring on a long string which the children in the circle held. Slyly the Irishmen passed the ring from neighbor to neighbor. Those who did not hold it moved their hands back and forth, pretending to be passing it. The poor inspector kept his eyes wide open and tried to guess who held the ring. His first two guesses were false, but on the third try he caught his Irishman, who then became the inspector. The second inspector was not so successful as his predecessor and guessed incorrectly three times. He had to choose a man to take his place. Every time an

inspector made a mistake, the children gave a wild whoop; and every time an Irishman was caught there was a groan.

Soon everyone had a chance to be the inspector, and Patty decided that the poor pig was tired of being chased, since after all perhaps he didn't belong in the parlor even if he was Irish.

TEARING SHAMROCKS

"But there is something that belongs in every Irish home," she added, "the shamrock. Lets see who can tear the best one." She gave each child a sheet of construction paper and asked him to tear out an outline of the national plant. As there were shamrock leaves all around the room, it was easy to make fair copies.

SHAMROCK FORTUNES

The children compared their shamrocks with those which Patty had made. The hostess explained that the "little folk who haunt the Emerald Isle" performed magic on hers and that each one had a fortune. She asked the boys and girls each carefully to take one from the curtains. She had her own marked in an out-of-the-way place.

There were shrieks of laughter as they read their fortunes to themselves. Patty asked the guests to gather again in a circle and share the news of their destinies with their friends.

"In 1956 you will be declared the greatest potato eater in your state."

"You will be a greater snake charmer than St. Patrick in thirty years."

"No one in the country will be as great a story teller as you in 1978."

Every fortune was so far fetched that no one could take offense.

At last Patty read hers. It said, "Hunger will make your friends very cross if you don't feed them soon."

REFRESHMENTS

To the strains of an old Irish tune, the guests marched into the dining room, where the table was centered with a large white cake with shamrocks on the frosting. Around it was a ring of green tapers in potato holders. Little clay pipes tied with green ribbons marked the places.

The children were served cottage cheese with a little green pennant on a toothpick stuck in its center, jelly sandwiches, hot chocolate, the cake, and mint ice cream.

SUGGESTIONS

This party is planned for boys and girls from eight to thirteen years of age. It may be given in any room that will accommodate eight or more guests. By dividing the children into groups of twelve, church and school classes may give the party with very few changes. The children may write the fortunes for each other before the party. Of course, they should be carefully censored so no sensitive child will draw an unpleasant fortune.

SAINT PATRICK

If there is time, after all the games here mentioned have been played, the children may see how many words they can get out of Saint Patrick, following the rules for "Valentine Greetings" (page 31).

They may also try to identify the "Ghost of the Emerald Isle," following the rules in the Halloween Party (page 131).

MATERIALS NEEDED

Invitations: Paper, crayons or paint, scissors, paste.

Decorations: Shamrocks, green candles in potato holders.

Games: Potato, smooth stone, handkerchief for blindfolding, small shamrock for each guest, ring on long string, construction paper to tear shamrocks, music, shamrock fortunes.

Favors: Musical potato, book of Irish jokes, clay pipes.

Peter Rabbit Party

PETER RABBITS, ALL DRESSED UP IN LITTLE BLUE JACKETS LIKE the one which the story book Peter lost under Mr. McGregor's fence, were sent to bear the invitations to Hilda Krantz's Easter party. Hilda's mother traced the picture of Peter, and Hilda colored the bunny with her own crayons. Then her mother wrote the invitation below the figure.

DYE EASTER EGGS

As each little girl arrived at Hilda's home, she was led into the kitchen, where large bowls of Easter egg dyes were set on the table ready for coloring eggs. One girl wanted a yellow egg, another a blue, and another a green. Hilda didn't have any green dye; so with her mother's help she mixed some of the blue and yellow in another bowl. Hilda's mother marked each egg with the name of the person who dyed it.

After an egg was all dyed and marked, Hilda escorted the guest back into the living room and gave her a puzzle of a bunny. While some of the guests were busy in the kitchen, others were occupied in the living room. At last Hilda asked her guests to put their puzzles back into their boxes and take them to the bedroom with their wraps. One little girl said she thought that was a funny place to keep puzzles; but Hilda replied that she believed it to be a rather convenient place, for her guests could take them home as favors from the party.

"Do you all know the story of Peter Rabbit?" asked Hilda's mother as she gathered the children around her.

"Of course," they answered.

"Remember the time Mr. McGregor chased him all about the garden?"

"That's the best part of the story," someone chuckled.

47

PLEASE COME TO MY
EASTER PARTY
MARCH 27, 3 O'CLOCK
HILDA KRANTZ
855 SHORE AVE
PLEASE REPLY

"We'll act out that part," said Hilda's mother. "Most of us are going to be part of the fence, and we'll form a wide circle with our hands joined and our arms stretched out as far as they can be."

"Now," she continued when the guests were in the circle, "you may be Peter and you may be Mr. McGregor." The two guests dropped out, and the hole in the fence was closed. According to directions, Peter ran in and out under the boards of the fence (the arms of the children) and between the fence posts (the guests themselves). She never crossed the circle nor ran to another part of the room, and Mr. McGregor followed right in her footsteps. The children couldn't help shouting as Peter dodged here and there, but at last she was captured and each girl chose a successor to run. This time Mr. McGregor just could not catch Peter; so Hilda's mother suggested that they turn about. Peter was caught. Again each chose a successor. Soon everyone had a turn; and as they were rather tired of running, Hilda suggested that they try to pin on Peter's tail, which he had lost in the hurry of the chase.

PIN THE TAIL ON THE BUNNY

Hilda gave each child a pin and a little paper tail while her mother hung on the wall a large sheet with a picture of the bunny. In turn each child was blindfolded, turned around three times, and then directed to pin the tail on the bunny. Poor Peter! He stood on tails and had them growing on his ears and at the end of his nose. Only once did anyone come anywhere near the spot where his tail should be.

"But," said Hilda, "that's what he gets for being such a naughty bunny and running away from home." She gave the little girl who had pinned the tail nearest to the marked spot a soft little bunny to keep.

FINDING PETER'S HOME

"You know," said Hilda's mother, "Peter really did go home after all. But his home was rather hard to find under a tree. Let's see, didn't you pin that tail on Peter's nose?" she asked a little girl. "I think that was a funny thing to do; so we'll let you be the first one to pretend to be Peter for this next game."

She explained the rules, which sounded like a new game of hide and seek, and the guests did as directed. All the children closed their eyes as Peter went to hide. The first Peter stood behind an open door. The children started to look for her—under the chairs, in the closets, every place in the big front room and the hall. They knew she wouldn't be in a hard place, but each wanted to be the first to see her. At last one girl spied Peter and very quietly sat down near by. Soon another guest found them and sat down. Before long, everyone was sitting in Peter's home, and the first who discovered the spot was Peter for the next game. The guests played the game several times with Peters choosing spots behind the screen, back of the big chair, and next to the grandfather's clock in the hall. One little Peter sat in the corner of the room where the guests were, just to see what they would do. Of course, she was spotted quickly, but the youngster who first sat next to her was chosen Peter.

REFRESHMENTS

"I'll show you another home," said Hilda after a time. "This time keep your eyes wide open and follow me." She led the guests into the dining room. In the center of the table was a big bunny sitting on a grass nest from which colored ribbons extended to each place. A little fluffy chicken sat astride each water glass, and the eggs which the children had dyed marked each place.

For supper the children were served rolled jelly, creamed cheese, and peanut butter sandwiches, carrot strips, hot chocolate, cookies, and—to remind them of Peter—a flower in a flower pot. Hilda didn't have to tell her friends that the small earthen pot was lined with wax paper, that the soil was chocolate ice cream, and the flower was made of gumdrops on a toothpick. The little guests had much better luck than Peter had with his pot. Not one tipped hers over.

50

After all the dishes were cleared away, someone wondered about the ribbons at the places. Hilda suggested that each person pull; and to the surprise of all, they discovered that the big bunny was sitting on a nest of tiny bunnies.

As the guests departed, Hilda gave each one a sack so that she might take home her puzzle, egg, little chicken, bunny, and flower pot.

SUGGESTIONS

Children from five to eight years of age—whether girls or boys or both—will enjoy this party, which may easily be given in a home of any size. If church classes and school groups are small, not more than twenty children, teachers may adapt these plans for their use.

If there is time for one more game, the children may play the bird and squirrel game in the Spring Party (page 67), calling the mother bird a mother duck, and the squirrels weasels which are trying to steal the eggs.

MATERIALS NEEDED

Invitations: Paper, pencil, crayons.

Decorations: Batten chickens, rabbit for centerpiece, flower pots, gumdrop flowers, ribbons.

Games: Egg dyes, hard-boiled eggs, bunny puzzles, picture of rabbit pinned to sheet, paper tails, pins, sacks.

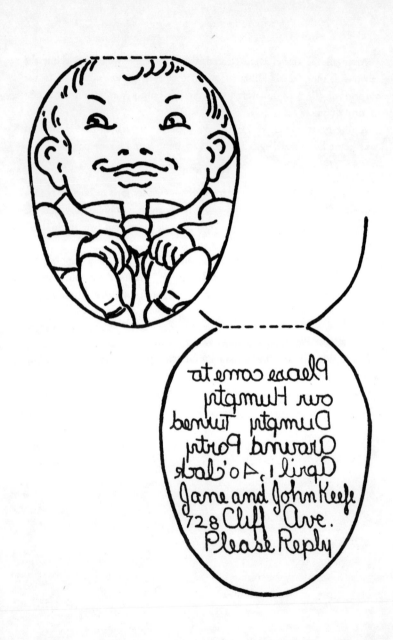

Please come to
our Humpty
Dumpty Turned
Around Party
April 1, 4 o'clock
Jane and John Keefe
728 Cliff Ave.
Please Reply

Humpty Dumpty Turned-Around Party

"Humpty Dumpty sat on a wall.
Humpty Dumpty had a great fall."

Woops! Everything was upside down and turned around. The invitations which Jack and Jane Keefe made for their Humpty Dumpty party certainly showed the effects of a tumble. The outside pictured Humpty in his original condition, but on the inside was queer writing which could be read only by holding the note before a mirror or against a light.

Jane made the drawings of Humpty while Jack turned his attention to the writing. First he wrote the invitation using a sheet of carbon paper with the inked side next to the original paper so that the copy appeared on the back of the first sheet. Then he traced the backward writing on the invitations Jane had started. The names and addresses were written plainly, and more than one little friend came to ask what it was all about.

As the guests arrived, they read a big sign on the front door which said, "Door Back Use Please." That was easy to figure out after deciphering the invitation. They scurried around to the rear entrance and were met and led to the basement to remove their hats and coats.

SACK MASKS

Jack quickly took each guest upstairs, where Jane pinned a number on his back and gave him the queerest mask ever made—a big paper sack with holes for eyes cut on one side and a grotesque face painted on the other.

"You'll have to follow your nose," she said, "and don't forget that your nose is on the back of your head."

MEETING BACKWARD PEOPLE

Then she explained that she would take him into the living room, and that as the other guests arrived she would like to have him walk backward, disguise his voice and posture, and fool everyone as much as possible. The guests certainly made a funny looking group as they squeaked and grunted at each other, tried to shake hands backward, and bumped into each other once in a while by mistake. When all were present, Jack passed out pencils and pieces of paper with numbers on them. The guests tried to guess the names of the other people present, but no one had a perfect score. Just to turn things around a bit, Jane gave a paper mask to the lad who had the most wrong. Each guest was allowed to keep his own sack mask.

MEETING BLIND PARTNERS

"I'd like you people to know just how twisted Humpty was as he rolled over and over during his fall," said Jack, as he and Jane divided the guests into two groups and lined them up on opposite sides of the room. The host asked them to count off and then had each take notice of who was his partner on the other side of the room. According to directions, each person closed his eyes, turned around three times, and tried to walk in a straight line and shake hands with his partner. The couples were certainly very well mixed up.

"Are you number 1?" asked a boy.

"No, I'm number 5," answered the little girl he had bumped into, keeping her eyes still closed.

"You won't do," said the boy as he went to try to find number 1.

Number 3's were the first to be joined and withdrew to one side of the room laughing and laughing as they watched the other guests trying to find their partners. Soon everyone was matched, and Jane asked them to line up again, not in the same order.

FEEDING BLIND PARTNERS

This time she gave each person on the west side of the room a spoon. They did exactly as they had done before only they had to pretend to feed their partners after they had matched them. Of course, no one touched a spoon except the one offered by his own partner.

The guests were again lined up. Jack gave clean spoons to the guests standing against the east wall and put a candy heart into each. Again neither a boy nor a girl could feed anyone until he had found his own partner. Several guests dropped their hearts, and were disqualified then and there; but two couples actually managed to get together. Jack gave boxes of animal crackers to the couple which won the first contest, boxes of cinnamon balls to those who won the second, and jars of candy sticks to those who won the third.

PIN THE TAIL ON THE DONKEY

"Here's an old donkey," said Jack, pinning the main portion of a traditional "pin the tail on the donkey" game on the wall. "He's been saying 'He Haw' all his life. Now we'll play a joke on him and try to pin the tail on his nose."

One by one the guests were blindfolded, turned around, and told to pin the tail on the animal's nose. One little boy wasn't listening and almost pinned the tail where it usually should be, but most of the children came rather close to the front of the beast. In fact, a little girl pinned the tail right smack on the tip of the nose; so Jack gave her the game as a prize.

BLIND ARTISTS

The guests were certainly surprised at the next feat they were asked to perform. They all sat down at a big table covered with newspapers. Each was given a piece of plain paper, crayons, and a rag with which to blindfold himself.

"I can't see to draw at all," said a little girl.

"Let's find out," said Jane. Of course, the pictures were very funny.

Some had trees growing on top of houses and little boys standing underneath flower beds with the wildest colors. Jane thought it remarkable that the guests could draw at all, and explained that those who couldn't draw well, at least had some excuse for their lack of talent. She started to make an art exhibit.

REFRESHMENTS

"Pardon me," said her brother. "Am I mixed up, or is it time for breakfast?" The guests assured him that it was time to eat whatever meal he wanted to call it. He invited them to come into the bedroom, where a table was set up in banquet style—or as he thought banquets should be served, with plenty of room for food and almost no decorations.

But there were place cards, peculiar, of course. The first initials of the names were interchanged so that Bob Jones' card read "Job Bones," and Jack's name was "Kack Jeefe."

A little tomato soup was served in a coffee cup followed by deviled eggs in sherbet glasses. Mashed potatoes and carrots were served on salad plates; and brown bread, covered with cream cheese to make it look like cake, was passed. White cake was cut in slices and frosted on the large flat surface to make it look like bread and butter; and the ice cream, in soup dishes, completed the menu.

As a parting gesture, Jane and Jack gave their guests horns and whistles, explaining that they thought it was New Year's Eve, but after all they were mixed up and turned around.

SUGGESTIONS

This party is designed for children from the ages of eight to fourteen, so that they may do most of the work themselves. Of course, as with any party, the plans will have to be adapted to fit the home in which it is given. If the bedrooms are too small, the supper may be served in the basement, or in any room except the dining room. Church and school groups may easily give the party, as the contests work equally well for large and small groups. They may want to have the guests make their own masks, as this will give them something to do upon arrival.

MIRROR CONTEST

If the party is large, it might be well to have part of the guests engage in a different contest as the remainder are pinning the tails on the donkey's nose. One at a time the boys and girls sit before a mirror and a leader holds a milk bottle over the contestant's head. At the side is a pan of peanuts. The contestant looks only at the glass as he picks up the peanuts and drops them into the bottle one at a time. The one who can drop the most into a bottle in two minutes wins a box of peanut brittle.

A contest of unscrambling words as described in the Frontier Party (page 150) would work well with this party theme. Names of animals might be used.

MATERIALS NEEDED

Invitations: Paper, carbon paper, pencil, coloring materials.

Decorations: Sign "Back Door Use Please," place cards.

Games: Heavy paper sacks made into masks with holes on one side and grotesque faces on the other, numbers, pins, paper and pencil for each guest, spoon for each guest, candy hearts, "pin the tail on the donkey" game, blindfold for each guest, paper and crayons for each guest.

Favors: Animal crackers, cinnamon balls, candy sticks, horns, whistles.

Cowboy Party

$\mathcal{E}$ I-KO-O-OH." IT WAS TIME FOR SPRING ROUNDUPS IN THE West, so "Rancher" Fred Stone sent cowboys to spread the word to his friends. He drew his figures on white paper, colored their clothes with gaudy paints, and wrote the invitations in the loops of the lassoing ropes.

He removed all the overstuffed chairs from the living room in his home where the party was to be given and substituted straight-backed chairs.

"A little more rustic," he thought. "Gives more room and is much easier on the furniture." He hung some skins he borrowed on the walls just to give atmosphere.

"I'm not just sure which ranch each of you came from," said Fred in all seriousness to his guests when they were assembled for the roundup; "but I'll give you these cards, and then you can get together in your own groups. Those from the **2-X** ranch can have this for their stamping grounds," he continued, pointing to one corner of the room, "and those from **T+O** can stand over here." The cards he handed out, each of which had a ranch brand on it, aided the boys in forming groups, which later proved to be relay teams. The cards were also large enough to use for keeping score.

BREAKING BRONCOS

"You know those broncos that we have let run all winter?" said Fred, assuming a wide stance and talking in a husky voice. "Our first job is to rebreak them. That's going to mean lots of twisting and turning before they will run a straight course."

He asked the guests to line up according to ranches in relay teams. He gave each leader a yardstick and instructed him to place both hands on top of it, put his head on his hands, turn around three times, run to the end

58

of the room and back, and give the stick to the next in line. It sounded "right easy," and the leaders started out; but sure enough, just as Fred said, it took a lot of twisting before they were running in a straight course. The other members of the teams gave the old cowboy yell, "Ei-ko-o-oh!" to cheer the leaders on. Each person had his turn to twist and run. The members of the team which first had its broncos tamed—that is, had each member run and return—put down a score of one on their cards. The second team put down two's.

LASSOING

As jumping through the ropes was the one part of trick lassoing that struck Fred's fancy the most, he gave each leader a big rope tied in a loop. At Fred's signal, each leader passed the loop over his own head, stepped out of it, and gave it to the next person in line, who did the same. Some of the boys became all tangled up, but they got out of it all right as the other guests laughed and shouted. The members of the winning team scored one as before, and the other team scored two's. By popular request, the relay was repeated, after which the scores were added. Members of 2-X ranch had the lowest scores.

Fred produced brightly colored handkerchiefs made of inexpensive cambric and gave the winners first choices. As the cowboys tied the kerchiefs around their necks, they looked much, much more like the pictured Westerners.

STOCK HUNT

"Of course," said Fred, "the roundup is the most exciting work that we do all year; but I don't want any of you ever to forget to be on the outlook for horses that have strayed and cows that are mired at the streams' edges. Now I am going to divide you into two groups and delegate one bunch to look for horses and one for cows."

Then the host went on to explain that there was an equal number of paper horses and cows hidden about the room. He appointed a captain for

each search squad. According to Fred's direction the boys started to look for their respective animals. Soon there was a loud "moo." Someone had found a cow. The captain rushed to the spot from which the cry was coming and put the animal in a little box corral he had. The cowboy did not move from the spot of his discovery until he had delivered the cow. In another corner of the room, there was a "whinnie." The captain of the horse crew dashed in that direction. First thing anybody knew there was a series of moos and whinnies; and the captains rushed madly about, first here and then there, collecting their animals so that the boys might continue their search. The boys searching for cows were very careful not to let anyone know when they saw a horse, and the horse hunters returned the compliment. At last Fred called time. The animals were counted, and there was one more animal in the horses' corral than in the cows'.

HUNTING

"I guess you boys deserve a day off to go hunting," said the head rancher. He suggested that they scurry around and help him place chairs in a row alternately facing opposite walls. Each boy sat on a chair, and Fred gave him the name of some article that a cowboy might take on a hunt, such as gun, rope, chaps, hat, saddle, sardines, blanket, and numerous other essentials. Fred named himself Bread and started to walk around the chairs, saying, "I am going hunting, and with me I shall take my gun." The cowboy named Gun jumped up and put his hand on Fred's shoulder and marched with him as Fred said, "I am going hunting, and with me I shall take sardines." Sardines jumped up and put his hand on Gun's shoulder and marched with the two. One by one, Fred called the names of all the articles and marched with them all

about the room. All of a sudden he said, "Bang!" The guests all ran for chairs, and so did Fred. Poor little Rope was left standing and became leader for the next game. But he liked marching around and calling all the names, and he was certain to get a chair the next time, for he knew just when he was going to say "Bang!" and was ready to run.

BIRD CALLS

Soon Fred noticed that his friends were getting tired and suggested that they sit down and pretend to be at the edge of a stream listening to wild bird calls. Chaps, the last to be left standing in the hunt game, stood blindfolded in the center of a circle of his fellow workers. He turned and pointed to one of the boys, who made a noise like a crow. Chaps guessed who made the sound, and that boy took the place in the center of the ring. He in turn pointed to another lad, who made a noise like a robin. Twice the pointer guessed, but each time he was wrong; so he choose a successor and took a place in the circle. Fred laughed and laughed as his friends imitated birds and was just as glad as he could be that he had never been in a forest where there was such a queer racket. Everybody had a chance to make a noise and to try to guess the names of the birdlike singers.

REFRESHMENTS

While the boys were still sitting in a circle, Fred suggested that they sing some cowboy songs and some old favorites too. Meanwhile, he went out into the kitchen and brought back what he called "hot buffalo steak" sand-wiches (hot roast beef), potato chips, ice cream, and cookies.

SUGGESTIONS

Boys—or boys and girls—from eight to twelve years of age will enjoy this party, which may be given in almost any room of fair size. School and church groups will find it fun to give with almost no alterations. In the hunt and identifying the birds, the directors would do well to divide the group into smaller groups of fifteen or twenty boys and girls.

DRESS FOR RODEO

If there is time for one more game, "dressing for the rodeo" will be enjoyed. Four chairs are placed in four corners of the room, and each bears a sign: shoes, kerchiefs, coats, hats. Six boys race at a time, and the host makes sure that each has the articles he needs. At a signal, the boys run to the first chair and remove their shoes, to the second and remove their kerchiefs, to the third and remove their coats, and to the fourth and remove their hats. Then they run around and put on each article of clothing as they reach that chair. This could also be worked out in relay fashion if the party is large.

If one more quiet game is needed, the guests might play "birds fly" as described in the Hobo Party (page 90).

MATERIALS NEEDED

Invitations: Paper, pencil, coloring materials.

Decorations: Animal skins.

Games: Yardstick for each relay team, rope tied in loop for each team, paper cows and horses, handkerchief for blindfolding, card with ranch brand on it for each guest, box corral for each team, chair for all but one guest.

Favors: Cambric kerchief for each guest.

ANNOUNCING A SPRING PARTY

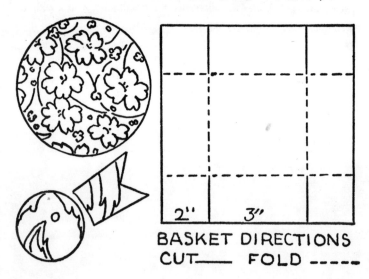

2"   3"

BASKET DIRECTIONS
CUT —— FOLD -----

Spring Party

As THE LITTLE BIRDS WENT HOP, HOP, HOP ABOUT THE YARD, Teddy Hack helped other little creatures hop right into envelopes as invitations for his spring party. His little birds didn't look just like the ones that were flying around outdoors; for Teddy, although he was only four years old, helped his mother make them out of left-over dress materials. For each invitation, Teddy cut out three pieces of material: a circle about three inches in diameter for the body, a circle about an inch and a half in diameter for the head, and a funny little forked piece for the tail. He pasted these in place on a sheet of paper and drew a beak and feet. His mother wrote the invitation below the figure.

Teddy remembered that his daddy always liked to tell all about egg hunts that he used to go on when he was a boy, and Teddy knew that his friends would enjoy this too. He made little nests by putting shredded paper into sauce dishes and filled them with many colored jelly beans, counting the same number of each color and then mixing them well.

No one could hunt for eggs, Teddy knew, without a basket; so he selected construction paper of the same colors as the eggs. His mother helped him cut a seven-inch square for each basket and mark off two inches from each edge. Teddy cut on the four vertical lines as far as the crossing horizontal lines and folded up the sheet on the lines of the inner square, thus making sides. He pasted down the overlapping portion to hold the sides in place. Then he made a handle by cutting a long strip of paper and pasting it firmly to two opposite sides.

Daddy had told Teddy that in the woods some nests are hard to find, but others are placed in plain sight. That was just the way he hid his sauce-dish nests with their brightly colored jelly-bean eggs.

65

After all of the eight little guests had taken off their wraps, Teddy gave each one a basket. His mother explained that the eggs were hidden around the room and that each boy or girl was to take out only the eggs that were of the same color as his basket. It wasn't hard to find the eggs, and it was a lot of fun picking out just the colors that belonged to each one. The children looked for their own and called to each other as they made a discovery. At last all the nests were found, and the boys and girls took their baskets to the room where they had put their wraps. One little boy accidentally tore his basket on the arm of a chair and spilled all his jelly beans; so Teddy gave him a new basket with clean eggs.

SUN AND SEEDS

Teddy's mother drew the children around her in a circle and asked them how many had watched little flowers grow. One little boy said that his father planted a garden, and just that morning a green blade appeared popping up above the ground. A little girl told how she watched her mother's ivy grow all winter, and ever so often a new leaf, much brighter green than the other leaves, appeared. Everybody there knew something about flowers and plants.

"What makes them grow?" asked Teddy's mother.

"The sun!" all the children said together.

Then Teddy's mother told them how to play "sun and seeds." Following her directions, the children formed a circle and knelt with their hands over their faces as if they were sleeping seeds. Teddy was the first "sun" and ran around the circle, suddenly touching one little "seed." The seed jumped up and chased the sun around the circle; but the sun was too fast for the seed and darted into the vacant place in the circle before he was tagged. The little seed became the sun and tagged a little girl. This time, as the sun rounded the circle, he wasn't as lucky and was tagged, and had to be the sun again. The children played the game again and again until everyone had an opportunity to be the sun.

66

Teddy's mother again gathered the little guests about her and asked them if they had ever seen birds make their nests, and then if they had ever seen the mother and father birds guard these nests.

"Why do they stay so close to home?" she asked.

"They have to keep the eggs warm," said one little fellow.

"They don't want anyone to take the eggs," ventured another.

"What might take the eggs?" asked Teddy's mother.

"I know," said the biggest boy present, "squirrels."

"Now this time all you little seeds are going to be squirrels and the sun is going to be the mother bird who will guard her nest," she explained. The squirrels formed a circle around the mother bird, who sat blindfolded on a chair with a dish of candy eggs at her feet. Teddy's mother pointed to one little boy, who tiptoed toward the chair. The mother bird heard him coming and pointed to him, and he had to return to the circle. The next little squirrel was so quiet that he was able to get an egg. He became the mother bird. He felt sure that he heard someone coming, and pointed. But he was only imagining things, for the squirrel was approaching from another direction.

A few of the children managed to get eggs, but not very many of them. Teddy made them all happy by giving them each one.

CONSTRUCTION PAPER WORK

"I made the invitations myself," said Teddy as he brought out construction paper, blunt scissors, and paste. "Would you like to make your own place cards?"

"What shall we make?" asked one little boy.

"I'll show you how to cut out flowers," said a little girl near him.

"I'm going to make birds like yours, Teddy, only using paper," remarked a little girl sitting near him.

Plenty of papers were quickly spread all over the floor, and soon the children were seated upon them busily cutting and pasting.

REFRESHMENTS

In the meantime, Teddy's mother was very busy in the kitchen making flowers for refreshments. She covered Holland rusk with cream sauce and then made a daisy on each by placing white strips of boiled eggs like the petals of a flower and putting the yolks in the center for the yellow part of the daisy.

Teddy called to her to come and see the place cards. She admired them and then picked them up and put them around the table. In a jiffy, the tots found their places.

With the daisy dish, Teddy's mother served hot chocolate and birds' nest cakes. These were little cup cakes with cocoanut frosting built up around the edges. In the center of each were three candy eggs.

SUGGESTIONS

Children from four to seven years of age will enjoy this party. The number of guests should be kept small so that the children will not become too excited.

BUTTERFLY

If the children finish these games early and it seems wise to play another, the hostess might suggest "Butterfly! Butterfly!" One child sits in the center of a circle of children who have their hands behind their backs. A brightly colored handkerchief which represents the butterfly is slyly passed from child to child as they chant,

"Butterfly! Butterfly! Where can you be?
Butterfly! Butterfly! Come to me!"

At the end of the chant the child in the center tries to guess who has the butterfly. If she guesses correctly, the holder takes the center place. If her guess is wrong, she must try again. If she is wrong three times, she chooses someone to go in the center.

Children of this age might also enjoy playing "Did you ever see a birdie fly this way and that?" played like "Did you ever see a dolly?" described in the Doll Party (page 143).

(page 143)

MATERIALS NEEDED

Invitations: Dress materials, paper, paste, pencil.

Games: Shredded paper for nests, candy eggs, sauce dishes, construction-paper baskets, construction paper, paste, scissors, blindfold, chair.

HEREBY NOTIFIED TO
REPORT FOR DUTY AS
A DETECTIVE TO HELP
SOLVE THE QUEER
CASE OF THE STEALING
OF THE PET FROG OF
MRS. PIRANA TITHERS.
REPORT SATURDAY
EVENING 7 O'CLOCK
AT MY HEAD QUARTERS

MICHAEL TRACY
8943 MARYLAND
AVENUE

Detective Party

OFFICIAL-LOOKING NOTICES, MARKED WITH SEALS, WERE SENT to Michael Tracy's friends to summon them to a detective party at his home where he said he wished them to solve the mystery of the stealing of the pet frog of Mrs. Pirana Tithers.

As the guests arrived, Mike did more than fingerprint them. He traced the outline of each left hand, numbered the paper with the drawing, recorded it, and kept its identity a secret.

IDENTIFYING HANDPRINTS

Before starting the solving of the queer case, Captain Mike explained that his detectives must pass several tests. He asked them to look at each other's left hand for several minutes, and then be seated. He gave each one a sheet of paper with numbers on it and then passed around the drawings of the hands, ruling that there could be no more showing of hands during the test. Nobody's memory was perfect, but everyone managed to put down a few good guesses. One boy actually recorded six correct answers; so Mike pinned a tin star on him and pronounced him chief assistant.

PRACTICE SHOOTING

"Now boys," said Mike, "I am quite sure that this case will be solved without bloodshed. Still I would not want to be responsible for sending men into the field without first testing their shooting ability." He set up an inexpensive marksmen's game made with guns that shot rubber plungers, and lined the boys up on the other side of the room. One by one they shot, as Mike recorded their scores. The lad who shot the highest score received the game as a prize.

"I think that there may be some queer things about this case," said Mike, "and you may have to depend upon your ability to recognize voices. In any case, it is well to be prepared." He divided his guests into two groups of equal numbers and asked one section to leave the room and decide upon a song to sing. Mike then lined up chairs on one side of the room, asked those guests remaining to sit in every other one, and blindfolded them. The absent group returned, seated themselves in the vacant chairs, and began to sing "Dixie." When the last line was finished, Mike asked each blindfolded detective to name the guest who was sitting at his left. Three guessed correctly and were unblindfolded. The singers again performed, and this time two more voices were correctly identified. Soon everyone was without a blindfold. The group which had stayed in the room made its exit while the detectives remaining were blindfolded. The second group of detectives was no more clever than its predecessor, but in due time the members recognized all the voices.

MYSTERY SOLVING

By this time Mike was sure that his crew of detectives were trained well enough to take the case. He explained the facts, which were very simple. Mrs. Pirana Tithers was a peculiar old lady, and her pet frog was stolen. It was the duty of the detectives to find out who did it and why.

Each person on the job was given a pencil and a sheet of paper. Around the room were all the clues, some of them extraneous, but most of them of some import and interest. All of the clues were written on paper and hidden, some in obvious places, and others in more secluded nooks, like at the edge of the rug.

As each detective found a clue, he put it back into its original place. Of course the crime was a humorous one, and the clues were very different from those usually found. Some of them read: "All the blinds were pulled, as the old lady did not like sunlight"; "The ice man hated frogs"; "The next-door neighbor said she saw the frog in the morning"; "A pair of red gloves was found near the frog's bed"; "Mrs. Tithers declared that she raised her frog from a tadpole."

When a detective thought that he had enough data for a report, he withdrew from the others and wrote it out. The solutions were very, very different, and all very funny. Mike gave two prizes, one to the guest who wrote what he considered the best report, and one to the guest who turned his in first.

REFRESHMENTS

After so much work, the detectives were ready to eat. Mike invited them to come into the dining room, where he served them a reporters' lunch. This lunch consisted of hamburgers with all the "fixings" and milk.

SUGGESTIONS

The more ingenious the host is, the more fun he will have in giving this party. Two or three children from the ages of nine to fourteen may get together to entertain their friends. They will have as much fun working out their clues as the guests will have in solving the mystery. The party also has the advantage of not requiring any running, and for this reason it may be given either in or out of doors at any time of year. Church and school groups will find it an easy party to give for a comparatively small number of children, not more than twenty-five.

The host may give the detectives the opportunity to select the best solution. He may give them pencils and paper and ask them to vote after he has read all the solutions, requesting them not to vote for their own.

PROFILE PRINTING

If the host wishes, he may draw profiles as well as hands. A sheet of white paper is fastened to the wall, and the subject stands between it and a bright light, thus casting a shadow. The host traces the outline of the profile, numbers it, keeping a record of each number. During the party, the detectives try to identify the profiles.

Invitations: Paper, ink, crayons or water colors. (The invitations may have seals of sealing wax with a real ribbon attached.)

Games: Clues written and hidden around the living room, paper and pencil with which to trace hands, paper and pencil for each guest, gun set with rubber plunger bullets, blindfolds for half the guests, chair for each guest.

Carnival Party

$\mathcal{W}$HAT ON EARTH ARE YOU MAKING WITH THOSE RED AND YELLOW paints?" asked Hank Davis' mother one August afternoon. "You look for all the world as if you were making carnival handbills."

"That's just exactly what I'm doing, Mother, making handbills for my carnival party. I thought I would draw up my plans and see what you thought of the idea."

Hank's mother certainly did like the idea, and how they laughed and chuckled as they thought of ways that they could make a party seem like a real carnival.

Hank's friends had never been to a carnival party and hardly knew what to expect. With keen anticipation, each secured a pencil stub and carefully hung on to the invitation; for the last sentence of the handbill read, "This ticket plus one pencil stub will admit one."

Hank appointed himself as barker number 1. When the guests began to arrive, he stationed himself behind an orange-crate stand and called, "This way, folks! This way! Come right in! Only one pencil stub and your ticket will admit you to the greatest carnival on earth."

BALLOON STAMP

At length he left his post and walked among his guests, calling, "Never mind the crowd, folks! Never mind the crowd! The more crowded the better!" He gave each guest a balloon and told them all what he wanted them to do. Each person blew up his balloon and tied one end of a string around it. The other end he tied to his ankle with about two feet of loose line. The object of the game was for each one to break all the balloons he could and still protect his own. Everyone had to stay in a certain portion

75

Don't miss
Carnival Party
June 10. Home
of Hank Davis
317 North Fir St.
3 o'clock
This Ticket plus
one pencil stub
will admit one

of the yard. Whenever there was a "pop," the owner of the burst balloon withdrew from the crowd and cheered the other guests from the side lines.

"Behold the winner!" called Hank as he held up the hands of the only guest whose balloon remained unbroken. "To the winner goes the whistle —the whistle, ladies and gentlemen, which started the game."

CORN GAME

"And now, ladies and gentlemen, step right this way for the old corn game," called Hank. Each guest was given a handful of corn kernels and a "bingo" board. Hank was again the official and called out number after number drawn from a box beside him. Each time he called a number, everyone finding it on his card covered it with a kernel of corn.

"Bingo!" called a boy in the group. He was the first one to have a row or column completely covered. Hank gave him a certificate with which he might later claim his reward. Again and again the game was played, until everyone had a "bingo" at least once.

All of a sudden, Hank called out, "Here are your prizes!" and tossed candy kisses—wrapped, of course—over the heads of his friends. How those boys and girls did scramble to pick up the candy, for each one could have all he could grab. When Hank saw one little girl looking mighty sad because she could get only two, he pulled her to the side and gave her some he had not thrown. She promised not to tell a soul.

While the guests were scrambling to pick up their kisses, Hank and a pal went over to the clothesline and hung up a sheet with the picture of a funny-looking man on it. Hank let his pal be barker for a change.

HIT THE FUNNY MAN

"Ladies and gentlemen! How's your old left arm? Try your chance on the funny man," he bellowed. Hank lined up his guests and each in turn tried to hit the figure with a tennis ball. Those who were right-handed had to throw with their left arms; and the left-handed guests threw with their right. After each toss, the thrower chased the ball for the next person in line. In true carnival fashion, each guest received a cane, and those who hit the figure of the man were allowed to tie ribbons to their canes.

MERRY-GO-ROUND

Music began to flow through an open window in the house. Large pieces of cardboard, each marked "horse," "zebra," or the name of some other animal, were placed in a circle about the yard for "merry-go-round," a game played like "musical chairs." There was one less cardboard than players. The boys and girls lined up on the outside of the circle and marched gayly about as a lively tune was being played. Suddenly the music stopped. Each guest quickly tried to jump on a cardboard, but one little boy was left standing on the grass. He picked up a cardboard as the game started again and withdrew to the side line to cheer the others. One by one the guests withdrew, and soon one little girl was alone in the center. She received a music box.

FREAK SHOW

A freak show with freakier freaks than ever joined a real carnival was the last attraction of the afternoon. The guests sat in a circle to make their own oddities. Each was given a piece of paper which had been divided into thirds. Every boy and girl drew the picture of the head of any animal, made dots where his work left off on the middle portion of the sheet, folded his third under, and gave the paper to the person to the left of him. Then each person drew the body of any animal on the second portion of the paper he was holding, made marks where his work left off, and again passed to the person on his left. On the third section, each guest drew the hind legs of an animal. And what an exhibit followed! One freak had the head of a mule, the body of a dachshund, and the hind legs of an elephant.

REFRESHMENTS

As the guests stood laughing and laughing at their queer creations, Hank set up his lunch counter, which he made of boxes and boards. "Hamburger, lady! Nice hot hamburger, sir!" he called. With the hamburger sandwiches, he served pink lemonade and ice cream cones.

SUGGESTIONS

This party may be given by clever boys and girls from eight to twelve years old. As it is designed for almost any number of guests, church and school groups as well as individuals may find it useful. Like a real carnival, it should be given out of doors. In case of rain, it may be transferred to a large attic, recreation room, or social hall. If the hall is not very large and there are many guests, it would be well to substitute contests of throwing beans into a pan, dropping shelled peanuts into a bottle, and tossing cards across a line for the balloon game. The balloons may be given as favors. If there is time, the guests might try to guess the number of beans in a half-pint jar, and they might play "ring toss" as described in the Robin Hood Party (page 84).

MATERIALS NEEDED

Invitations: Paper, red and yellow paints or crayons.

Decorations: Boxes, counter of board and boxes.

Games: Balloon and three feet of string for each guest, whistle, bingo game, corn, certificates, tennis balls, picture of a funny man and sheet with line to hang it on, circles of cardboard marked with names of animals, musical instrument, pencils and paper for freak show.

Favors: Kisses, music box, canes, ribbons.

Robin Hood Party

$\mathcal{W}$ITH A "HEIGH HO, DERRY, DERRY, DOWN!" A STURDY MEMBER of Robin Hood's band, all dressed in coat and hat of green, stepped forth to summon merry men and maids to Sherwood Forest. In this case, he was made of paper and came out of an envelope in the mail to invite each guest to Phil Harper's Robin Hood party. All the details were written on the arrows, which could be withdrawn from the quiver slung over his shoulder.

Phil's own yard with its one big elm and two spreading basswood trees became the forest where the friends gathered as members of Robin Hood's band. Phil gave each one a slip of paper on which was written the name of one of the members of the famous outlaw group (or a name which might have belonged to one of them, for no book lists all those who joined Robin Hood, and Phil had a lot of fun imagining what unmentioned characters might have been called). Each guest pinned his name to his blouse and went around greeting his friends as "Hi, Little John. Hi, Friar Tuck. Hi, Maid Rowena. Hi, Maid Marian."

ROBIN HOOD AND THE SHERIFF

"Now, my merry, merry men," said Phil, "we'll play the game of 'Robin Hood and the sheriff of Nottingham.' You be Robin Hood," he continued as he pointed to one of the guests, "and the rest of us will be the sheriff's men." Following this explanation, the sheriff's men stood in a circle with their hands behind them, and Robin ran around and tapped one on the hands. This one immediately chased Robin around the circle, while the other guests laughed and shouted as the outlaw narrowly escaped the hands of the law by darting into the vacant place. The sheriff's man then became

Robin Hood, and he too was able to round the circle and get back into the vacant place before he was tagged. But the third Robin Hood was not so fortunate. He was caught and thrown into jail in the center of the ring. The game was played again and again, some outlaws gleefully getting away, and others being penned up. At last there were so many men in jail that the circle was really too small for fun; and since everyone was tired of running, Phil suggested that they turn to a new game.

ROBIN COMES

Once again the guests all became men of Sherwood and sat down in a circle as if waiting for their leader to come. "I'll start the game," said Phil. "It's played a great deal like 'bird, beast, or fish.' I'll say, 'Robin comes,' point at one of you, and count to ten. You must tell me how, or when, or where he comes before I stop counting, or else you will have to take my place in the center."

The first little boy at whom Phil pointed said, "Gladly." A little girl said, "Now." The third guest was going to say, "Softly," but couldn't think of it quickly enough; so she took Phil's place. Since not many were caught, the game was made harder.

The one in the center gave the name of a letter after saying, "Robin comes." He said, "Robin comes—R" and the one at whom he was pointing said, "Running," before the count of ten was reached. Whenever an outlaw couldn't think of a word, Phil said, he had the right to ask the questioner of what he was thinking; and as an answer had to be given, nobody said, "Robin comes—X."

When one little girl said, "Soft," rather than "Softly," the others corrected her, but let her answer count just the same, for they all knew that they would probably make mistakes when they were thinking so rapidly. Robin came "quickly, slowly, awkwardly, immediately"; in fact, he seemed to arrive in almost every manner and at every time that anyone could imagine, until at last Phil said, "Well, I guess Robin's here, all right. Let's let him try to escape the sheriff again and play 'join Robin now.'"

"Join Robin now" was played like "last couple out," with one guest as sheriff and the remainder of the group as men of Sherwood. The "men of Sherwood" were paired off and stood behind each other in a double line. The sheriff took his place at the head of the line with his back to the rest of the group. In a lusty voice this trusty guardian of the law bellowed, "Join Robin now!" The last couple in the line separated, each person running down his side of the line and out in front of the group to join his partner. The sheriff was not allowed to look behind him nor to run back of the place where he was standing; but the minute he saw an outlaw pass him, he gave chase. The first time the game was played, the two outlaws joined hands before either was tagged. They took their places as the first couple in the double line, and the sheriff again stood with his back to the group.

"Join Robin now!" again he called. This time he was able to catch one man; so he and the other runner became the first couple in the double line, and the captured victim became the sheriff. After everyone had had a chance to run, Phil and his partner slipped away from the others and set up two targets in another part of the yard.

SHOOTING TOURNAMENT

With ceremony, traditional of the days of King John, Phil blew a horn and formally announced, "Hear ye, one and all. A shooting tournament is about to begin. Will all of those standing in the left line march before this target, and all those standing in the right line march before this one?"

Then with dignity he gave the rules: each leader was to be given a bow and three arrows; at a signal they were to advance to the spots on the lawn which he had marked, shoot, and remain standing until another signal was given; together they were to march to the targets, pick up the arrows, and give them to the next in line.

The signal was given, the leaders shot, and the crowd cheered loudly. Phil carefully recorded the total score made by each. Each marksman had his chance; some missed the board completely, but two men made a bull's-eye. The members of the team which had the highest score received feathers dyed bright blue; and all the others received red feathers. The two guests with the highest individual scores were awarded the bow and arrow sets.

A feast, spread right out under the two basswood trees of Phil's Sherwood Forest, rounded up the festivities for the day. Heigh ho! What a merry time it was! The table of rough boards, set on sawhorses, was decked with green leaves. The menu included bacon sandwiches, fresh fruit, iced fruit juices, and ice cream cones.

SUGGESTIONS

Boys and girls from eight to twelve years of age will enjoy giving this party. It must take place outdoors or in a large social hall. Church and school groups will find it easy and fun to give. It will tie up well with teaching the English tales of Robin Hood, and the game "Robin comes" may help drive home the meaning of adverbs. Directors will find that they will have the greatest success if they will divide the classes into groups of from eleven to seventeen boys and girls.

RING TOSS

If the host does not wish to get bow and arrow sets, he may test his friends' skill by having them toss jar rubbers over a stick stuck in the ground. The guests are divided into groups and each leader is given five jar rubbers. The contest may continue with the same fanfare as described in the party plan.

The men of Sherwood would also like to identify bird calls as described in the Cowboy Party (page 62). The guests should be divided into small groups of about ten guests for this.

Invitations: Paper, pencil or pen and India ink, scissors, paints.

Decorations: Garlands of leaves for the table, boards, sawhorses.

Games: Slips of paper with names of characters from Robin Hood stories, pins, bow and arrow sets, pencil and paper for recording scores.

Favors: Red and blue feathers.

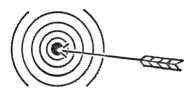

Hobo Party

GREATLY AS THEY DESIRED IT, JACK BROWN AND HIS PALS couldn't become tramps and wander about the country asking for handouts. But they could, and they did, become hoboes for a day at the party which Jack gave in his yard.

For each invitation, Jack drew a picture of a boy about his own age and wrote the invitation next to it. On the other side he scribbled, "Be sure to wear a hobo outfit."

The boys certainly did dress like hoboes. Jack thought that his rags and tatters were very funny until he saw his pals all dressed up in the clothes their dads and uncles had discarded. The games at the party were played out of doors; for, Jack explained, this is always a hobo's home.

HANDOUT

"We're goin' to play 'handout' first," Jack told his guests in a rough tone he adopted for the occasion, "because all you guys know that the first thing we have to think about is somethin' to eat." He then explained that the game was played something like "pussy wants a corner." One boy was chosen to be the hobo, and each of the other guests became a homeowner and was given a tree or marker to be his home.

The hobo went to a home and said, "Have you some food for a poor hungry man?"

The homeowner said, "Next-door neighbor."

The hungry hobo walked from home to home and each time was given the same answer.

Suddenly he called, "Everybody out." The homeowners all changed places, and the hobo slipped to a marker before a new homeowner could reach it. The homeowner left without a home became the next hobo and the game was played again and again.

CRACKER LUNCH

After so much begging, Jack thought the hoboes deserved some lunch. He gave each guest three crackers. At his signal, the guests began to eat them as quickly as they could. The hobo who finished first, whistled, and at the same time thumbed for a ride, won the game and was given a bright red handkerchief in which to carry his lunch in the future.

COP AND TRAMP

Sleeping on benches, Jack explained, is often the fate of hoboes; and not one of them likes to be awakened by an unsympathetic policeman. He selected the winner of the last game to be the first hobo for "cop and tramp." Each time the game was played the hobo sat with his hands covering his face as if he were sleeping. The other guests, policemen, stood in a line behind him. One lad at the end of the line started to tiptoe toward the tramp, who heard him coming and pointed to him. The policeman returned to his place in the line. No one moved for a minute, but the tramp thought he heard a sound and pointed. He was forced to give up his bench to another tramp who decided to be more cautious. In fact, he was so cautious that he did not point to the next policeman, who actually reached the bench, tagged the tramp, and took his place. The game was repeated several times.

NEW HOBO

All the guests agreed with Jack that hoboes never stay in one place very long, and that as one enters a town, another is very apt to be leaving it. The game next played was like "three deep." One guest was chosen to be the new hobo and another to be a policeman who was chasing him. Jack asked his guests to count off by twos and to form two concentric circles with the number 1's outside. Then he asked each number 1 to stand behind a number 2 and then spread out with a space between each couple. The

87

hobo and the policeman started their race, and the hobo ran around the circle and dodged in front of two people. The boy on the outside ran as the policeman pursued him, and caught him. Each chose a successor.

The hoboes soon realized that they had much better chances to escape when they ran only short distances; and the game was much more exciting that way, for more people were running more of the time. In fact, the changes were made so quickly, and everyone had so many chances to run that they soon became tired, and Jack suggested that they all sit down and tell about their trips.

ALPHABET TRIPS

The hoboes sat in a circle, pretending to be gathered around an open fire. One boy began the game by saying, "The place I like best is Albany." (He choose a city starting with the letter "A.") The next hobo said, "The places I like best are Albany and Boston." The game continued, each person in turn repeating all that had been said and adding the name of a city whose first letter began with the next letter of the alphabet. Whenever anyone made a mistake by forgetting the name of a city or by getting it in the wrong order, he dropped out of the game. The hobo with the best memory, the one who stayed in the game the longest, was given a mouth organ with which he entertained his pals around the imaginary fire.

REFRESHMENTS

At the close of the afternoon, the young hoboes were ready for honest-to-goodness handouts. Jack passed all kinds of sandwiches and cakes which the tramps piled high on their paper plates. Fruit juices served in paper cups completed the refreshments.

SUGGESTIONS

This party may be given in a yard, a park, or on a beach by boys, or boys and girls from eight to twelve years of age. If it is given at a park or on a beach, a real fire might be built, around which the hobes could roast weenies rather than have the refreshments mentioned. School and church groups would find the party easy to give. The guests should be divided into groups of not more than fifteen players for "handout," "cracker lunch," "cop and tramp," and "alphaphet trips," and in groups of not more than thirty players for "new hobo." In case of rain, a church or school group could give this party in a recreation hall. An individual could give the party in his home if he asked his guests to sit on chairs in a circle when playing "handout," and if he substituted "birds fly" for "new hobo."

BIRDS FLY

The young host explains that hoboes live out of doors so much of the time that they learn a great deal about birds and animals. One hobo stands in front of the group, flaps his arms like wings, and says, "Robins fly; pigeons fly; sparrows fly." The other guests do as he does as long as he gives the name of a bird. But if he says, "Dogs fly," or gives the name of any creature which does not fly, anyone who makes the motion of flying must drop out. The last person to be eliminated wins the game.

The guests might also play "constellation," as mentioned in the Skipper Party (page 95).

MATERIALS NEEDED

Invitations: Paper, pencil or pen and India ink, crayons or paints.
Games: Markers for "handout," three crackers for each guest, chair.
Favors: Red handkerchief, mouth organ.

Skipper Party

SHIP AHOY! SHIP AHOY! A LITTLE SKIPPER STOOD AT THE wheel of the good ship "Morgen" ready to take Jimmy's little friends on an afternoon jaunt. The skipper was drawn on paper at the head of an invitation, and the jaunt was Jimmy's skipper party.

After the invitations were mailed, Jimmy found that he could do a great many things to get ready for his party. He decided to give each guest a little walnut-shell ship that would really float. To make each one he cracked a walnut in two, took out the meat, and painted the shell a lovely pastel shade with water colors. The sail was a triangular piece of construction paper pasted to a match-stick mast. Mast and sail were held in place with a little candle wax dropped into the bottom of the shell.

No skipper party would be complete without fish, thought Jimmy; so to make sure that each guest would get one, he made brightly colored fish for place cards. He traced pictures on stiff paper and then painted them all the colors he had seen on pictures of fish (and quite a few he just imagined).

He remembered that his Aunt Edyth had bought some licorice sticks in the shape of anchors when he had visited her the year before. He tried to get some at the neighborhood store; but as they didn't carry them, he bought plain licorice sticks instead. He tied long strings of equal lengths on these for an anchor-pulling contest.

To get ready for a fishing contest, he procured a stick about fifteen inches long, tied a string to one end of it, and tied a hook to the end of the string.

Next he made a ring toss deck game just like the one he had seen at his cousins'. He took a large board, about three feet by four feet, and pounded in nails a little way in systematic order. Each nail was marked a certain count with numbers clipped from an old calendar.

91

SKIPPER PARTY
JULY 18, 3 O'CLOCK
JIMMY MORGEN
737 FOREST ST.
PLEASE REPLY.

The last thing he did before the party was to make waves for his table setting. He merely cut strips of crepe paper one inch wide in continuous half circle designs. Each strip was as long as the bolt of paper.

Some of the guests arrived a little early; but at the stroke of six bells, three o'clock at sea, the party began.

PULL ANCHORS

"First of all we'll pull anchors," said young Jimmy as he passed out his licorice sticks with strings attached. According to his directions, the guests put the free ends of the strings in their mouths, stood with their hands behind their backs, and at the sound of eight bells, began to chew the strings. Three of the guests dropped theirs before they were hardly started. They had to pick up the strings and start again. Another little boy thought he could go faster if he used his hands, but Jimmy put a stop to that and asked him to start again too. The guests chewed and chewed, and no accidents happened until one little girl happened to look at a fat little fellow who was getting redder and redder in the face. She thought he looked funnier than all the other guests put together, and she laughed right out loud. Plop! Her anchor fell on the floor. At last one of the boys actually managed to get his anchor up, and he was awarded a little ship with two sails. Everyone was allowed to eat his candy, except those who had dropped theirs. But even they did not go hungry, as Jimmy gave each a new stick.

BIRD, BEAST, OR FISH

"We're headed for the open sea. What do you see, bird, beast, or fish? Supposing you be the first fisherman," said Jimmy, pointing to the guest who had won the last game. "The rest of you form a circle, please."

The fisherman, standing in their midst, said, "Bird, beast, or fish—*bird,*" pointed to a little girl, and counted ten.

Quick as a wink the little girl said, "Sea gull."

The fisherman had to try again. "Bird, beast, or fish—*fish,*" he said, pointing to the fat boy.

"Trout," said the lad without a moment's hesitation.

Again the fisherman tried. "Bird, beast, or fish—*beast*."

A little girl said, "Dog"; but since she was so slow that the young fisherman reached the count of ten before she spoke, she took his place. The game was played this way for several minutes, and then it was made harder. No one was allowed to give the name of anything that had previously been mentioned. This made many, many changes. Soon everyone had a turn to be fisherman, and Jimmy told his guests that they might really go fishing.

FISHING

He brought out the little pole, onto which he had tied the string and hook. A dishpan containing fifteen or twenty rubber bands was placed on the floor and a chair set in front of it with its back to the pan. Each child in turn knelt on the chair and fished for the bands. Jimmy kept time carefully so that each child had exactly five minutes in which to fish. Every time a fisherman made a catch, the other guests counted out loud and the score was recorded. When Jimmy looked at the scores, he discovered that there was a tie between a little boy and a girl. They tried again, and the boy hooked one more band. He was given a book about ships.

DECK RING TOSS

After fishing, the young guests joined in a game of deck ring toss. Jimmy brought out the board which he had made and directed the guests to line up so that each might have five turns at throwing rings. He gave each one five quart jar rubbers as he was about to throw. The first little boy landed his on fifteen at his first toss; his next ring fell on the floor; and the next ones gained him five each. He added up his score as the others helped him. After everyone had a turn, Jimmy made the score harder, and more fun. He wrote "ouch" on a piece of paper and pasted it under one of the center nails. Every time anyone threw a rubber on "ouch" he lost all the score he had made at that point. The guests got more and more excited, but their game stopped when a bell rang—the call to supper.

With oh's and ah's the guests viewed the nautical scene in the dining room. The tablecloth was a blue cellophane sea with white crepe-paper waves running across it. The brightly colored fish bobbed up at each place, and the walnut-shell boats seemed to be anchored beside the water glasses.

The supper was a fisherman's delight of salmon loaf, green beans, mashed potatoes, dark brown-bread sandwiches, and ice cream.

SUGGESTIONS

Boys and girls from seven to eleven years of age will like this party. There may be from six to twelve guests. Of course, it may be used for a larger gathering if the guests are divided into small groups.

CONSTELLATION

If the guests finish with all the games before suppertime, they may enjoy playing "constellation." Each guest is given a pencil and paper and asked to draw five stars anywhere on the sheet. Then he is asked to imagine that this is a constellation and to draw a figure around the stars, very much as the ancient people did.

"Ship's cargo," as described in the Pirate Party (page 140), may also be played. The guests might say, "I pulled up my fishing net, and in it I found—"

MATERIALS NEEDED

Invitations: Paper, pencil or pen and India ink, water colors.

Decorations: Cellophane tablecloth, crepe-paper waves, walnut-shell ships, fish place cards.

Games: Licorice stick with string for each guest, short pole, string, hook, rubber bands, jar rubbers, board for deck game, nails, calendar, numbers, pencil, paper, paste.

Favors: Sailboat, book on ships.

Mother Goose Party

*L*ITTLE BO PEEP FOUND HER SHEEP, BUT WHAT FUNNY TAILS they had wagging behind them! At least the sheep that Jane Cole sent as invitations to her Mother Goose party had most peculiar tails.

For each invitation, Jane's mother traced a picture of Bo Peep and her lamb, but the poor little animal had nothing to wag. She wrote an invitation on a sheet of paper one and one-half inches by two inches, rolled it up quite small, and inserted it in a slit in the picture just where a tail should be. Jane colored Bo Peep's dress and put the invitation in an envelope ready to mail. Imagine the surprise that the little boys and girls had when they saw a sheep, even a paper one, whose tail came off to reveal such wonderful news.

BO PEEP AND HER SHEEP

When the guests arrived at the party, they talked of little else than Bo Peep and that sheep, so Jane told them about a game with those two characters. One little boy was chosen to be a lamb, and a little girl was chosen to be Bo Peep and was blindfolded. The remaining children formed a circle around the two characters. Bo Peep called out, "Here, lambie, lambie!" The sheep answered, "Ba, ba!" Bo Peep tried to move closer to the sheep, calling again and again. The sheep was not allowed to run, but he did his best to dodge his blindfolded mistress as she followed his voice around inside of the circle. At last she caught him, and each chose a successor. One little Bo Peep tried and tried, but she couldn't catch her sheep; so Jane let her and her sheep choose successors anyway. The game was repeated until at last everyone had a chance to be either little Bo Peep or the bleating lost sheep.

MOTHER—
GOOSE PARTY
AUG 10TH,
3 O'CLOCK
JANE COLE
1015 SOUTH
AVENUE
PLEASE REPLY

A picture of Little Miss Muffet, sitting on a tuffet, had been clipped from a Mother Goose book and pinned to a cloth on the wall. Jane gave each guest a little paper spider and a pin. In turn each child was blindfolded, turned about three times, and asked to pin his paper spider where it should go on the picture. There were spiders in Miss Muffet's hair, spiders on her shoes, and—horrors of horrors—spiders in her curds and whey! But one little boy pinned his spider almost on top of the one in the picture. He was given a big Mother Goose book as a prize.

JACK BE NIMBLE

After the first guest had pinned his spider on the picture, he was taken into another room to play, "Jack be nimble, Jack be quick. Jack jump over a pillow." In this room pillows were placed in a straight line three feet apart. Jane explained that she would blindfold the guest; her sister Molly would turn him around three times; and then he should jump over the pillows. The little guest wanted time to calculate the distances, and Jane gave him all the time he needed. As she blindfolded him, she talked to him all the time, asking him if he could see anything, and if he remembered just how far he would have to jump. Molly quietly removed the pillows and then turned him about. The jumper took one big jump and was relieved to think that he had not hit a thing. The next jump was successful too. In fact, he could hardly believe it when he made all the jumps just as he had hoped he would. When the blindfold was removed, he was quite put out to think how he had been fooled. But what fun he had seeing the joke played on all the other guests!

SALLY WATER

"Because you didn't see the joke played on anyone else, we'll let you be the first Little Sally Water," Molly said to the little girl who had last tried to jump the pillows. All the boys and girls formed a circle about the one chosen to be Sally, who knelt as the others walked around her chanting:

"Little Sally Water,
  Sitting in a saucer,
Crying and weeping for a nice young man.
  Rise, Sally, rise.
  Wipe out your eyes.
Turn to the east, turn to the west,
Turn to the one that you love best."

Sally rose when she was directed to do so, and the children stood still.
She kept her eyes closed and turned about as told with her hand out-
stretched. When the children finished the last word of the song, she
stopped, opened her eyes, and discovered whom she loved best, a little boy
with freckled nose. He stood in the center of the circle as the children
sang, "Little Tommy Water." He happened to point to the first little Sally,
so she just laughed and chose another friend to take her place. Before long,
everyone had a turn and the game ended.

TOMMY TUCKER

Little Tommy Tucker sang for his supper, and Jane allowed her guests
to do the very same thing. The last little girl to be Sally sang "Jesus Loves
Me," for she had learned it in Sunday school. The freckled boy sang
"Jackie Frost" that he had learned in school. As each performed, Jane let
him put his hand into a big bag and pull out a packet of sandwiches. A tap
dance was presented by a little girl with yellow curls; and a husky lad in a
dark brown suit said he would rather recite than sing, and recite he did,
"Jack and Jill."

Before long everyone had entertained in one way or another, except
the very smallest girl at the party. She just didn't know how to do anything, she said—that is, anything all by herself.

"Let's sing together then," said Jane. "We all know 'Rock a bye baby.' "
The tune wasn't quite the same tune that most teachers know, but everyone
joined in, so the little girl could claim her supper.

She helped Jane spread paper tablecloths on the bare floor, around which the youngsters squatted. The young hostess also brought in fruit juices and buckets of ice cream for each guest.

But the surprise of the afternoon was a great big pie, made from a dishpan covered with crepe paper, with brightly colored strings emerging from its center. Jane put her pie right in the center of one tablecloth and called the little friends to gather around, giving each one a string. When the strings were pulled, the pie opened; and out came all manner of noise makers. The "four and twenty blackbirds" baked in the old Mother Goose pie couldn't have made one bit more racket than the boys and girls did as they blew and blew their horns and whistles at the end of Jane's party.

SUGGESTIONS

The Mother Goose Party is planned for children from four to seven years of age. It would be well to limit the number of guests to about ten, as little children become quite confused when a large crowd is present. Of course, a child four years old cannot take the full responsibility of acting as host, but he can help at every point in this party, as the games are all old familiar ones which do not need much supervision.

LUCY LOCKET

If few of the children know "Little Sally Water," it would be hard to teach it to them at this time; but if several know it, the others can easily follow. A game of "Lucy Locket lost her pocket" might be substituted. The pocketbook, a very small one, is put in plain sight in the room. Music is played as the children search for it. It grows louder as someone is near the object and dimmer as all draw away. As soon as anyone sees the object, he sits down without saying anything. The game continues until everyone has seen it.

If there is time, the children might play "Jack Frost and the flowers" as described in the Snow Party (page 26).

Invitations: Paper, crayons, scissors, pencil.

Decorations: Paper tablecloths, paper bags for lunch.

Games: Pillows, paper spiders, picture of Miss Muffet pinned to a sheet, two handerchiefs for blindfolding, pins, pie made of dishpan covered with crepe paper.

Favors: Noise makers, Mother Goose book.

Indian Powwow

"K I YI! KI YI!" CALLED TED BRADFORD AND HIS TWIN BROTHER Terry as they ran around town delivering the invitations for their big powwow. Brave warriors, setting suns, sacred birds, and fish were all pictured in bright colors on the notes the boys had made of heavy brown paper, which looked at least somewhat like birch bark, or possibly like a scrap of buckskin.

"Blub," said Ted as he greeted each guest at the door of his home. It might have meant "hello" in some Indian language. "I am Brown Deer," he continued, pointing to a slip of paper pinned to his shirt. "Who are you?"

"Fleet of Foot," said the first guest.

"Write here. Pin here," directed Brown Deer, pointing again as he spoke. "Blub," he repeated, greeting the next guest who approached the door. "Who are you?"

"I don't know," said the little girl.

"Swan Maiden," Brown Deer told her. "Write here. Pin here."

Soon all the guests were going about saying, "Blub, Little Dove. How are you?"

"Blub, Spreading Eagle, fine."

Terry, self-termed Mighty Rock, gave each guest a headband, which unfortunately had no feathers. When the guests complained, the young brave explained that it was the duty of each warrior present to win the feathers if he could.

"We are gathered today for a big powwow," said Brown Deer, addressing his fellow warriors. "Let us form a council ring and count off into tribes."

After the tribes had been formed, Mighty Rock stood before the assembled groups and explained again that it was the duty of each warrior to win as many feathers as he could. This would, he said, be accomplished by showing skill in a number of relays which would give each brave an opportunity to win honor for himself and for his tribe.

RED MAN WALKING RACE

The guests were lined up in tribes on one side of the room for a "red man's walking race." As Brown Deer and Mighty Rock beat dishpan tom-toms, the chieftain of each tribe crossed the room in Indian fashion, one foot directly in front of the other with heel touching toe. When he reached the wall, he turned, and came back to his tribe in the same fashion, as all the other Indians let out wild war whoops to cheer him on. The chieftain touched the next in line, who walked in like manner as rapidly as he could and returned to tap the next person in line. The relay continued until the chieftain was again at the head of the line. He let out a whoop, louder than the whoops of all his warriors put together; and each of the members of the tribe which finished first received a feather for his band.

SHOOTING

"Big Indian must have good eye. Him must shoot good," said Brown Deer as he gave each chieftain three bean bags and placed a target on the floor in front of each line of Indians. Each target was made of the bottom portion of a big cardboard box with a medium-sized box pasted in its center and a small box pasted inside that, forming three "rings" in which the bean bags could fall. Brown Deer explained that a bean bag in the outer box would score ten points, in the middle box twenty points, and in the center box fifty points. Each redskin threw in turn. The one receiving the highest score was given three feathers, and the members of the team with the highest total score each received one feather. The young braves liked the contest so well that it was repeated twice.

ANIMAL HUNT

An animal hunt, with animal crackers as prey, was the next on the program. Each tribe was given its own campgrounds, and the Indians

BIG POW WOW
SATURDAY 4, O'CLOCK
CAMP BRADFORD
PLEASE REPLY

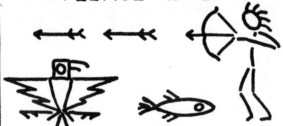

were told that they could bring only one animal into the grounds at a time. To enforce this ruling, a chieftain of each tribe was appointed referee in an enemy's camp. One stealthy warrior who tried to disobey the regulations found that his prey was captured and given to the warrior who was watching his grounds. After the redskins had spent fifteen minutes gathering animals from behind books, under chairs, and on window sills, the tom-tom was sounded and the count made. Members of the tribe which found the most animals each received one feather.

CORN RELAY

"Indians must take good care of corn," said Brown Deer, as he directed his guests to form in lines again for a corn relay. Before each chieftain he placed a dish of shelled corn. As the tom-tom started to beat, the chieftain picked up one kernel of corn and passed it to the Indian behind him, who in turn gave it to the next in line. Each warrior had to touch the corn; and when it reached the end man, he gave the whoop of his particular tribe as he deposited the kernel in the dish near him, and the leader started another kernel down the line. The team which first had all its kernels in the dish at the end of the line received feathers. Members of the losing teams were sure that they would win if the relay was repeated, so it was; and, sure enough, they did win on their second opportunity, and each brave received a feather.

STRINGING BEADS

"Now we string beads," said young Mighty Rock. The Indians squatted on the floor; and each was given a tiny dish containing beads, a needle, and a thread. When the tom-tom started to beat, the redskins started to string their beads. A little girl, who always made all her own doll clothes, finished long before the others did and was given three feathers; but even the most clumsy of the little boys kept stringing and stringing. As a reward, Brown Deer gave each guest five more feathers, and allowed each to keep the beads he had strung.

105

With five more feathers in the headbands, each and every guest looked like a real redskin and acted like one too, yipping and whooping around. Only by beating the tom-tom very loudly could Mighty Rock and Brown Deer quiet the Indians to let them choose their chief, the man who had the most feathers. With great ceremony, the young hosts led him to a table where there were favors with Indian designs piled around a little wigwam centerpiece. The chief received first choice. The members of the tribe which had won the most relays received next, but everyone was given an Indian favor.

REFRESHMENTS

Brown Deer and Mighty Rock soon made the Indians forget all about their contests as they brought in roast beef sandwiches (bear meat, they called it), carrot strips (wild roots), and ice cream (wild rice and honey).

SUGGESTIONS

This party may be given by boys and girls from eight to fourteen years of age. Church and school groups will find that the relays are simple and easy to direct. As the relays are all of a quiet nature—that is, do not require running—the party may be given almost anywhere, in a living room, a recreation room, a hall, or outdoors. If it is given outdoors, it would be fun to sit around a campfire to eat, and hamburgers might take the place of roast beef.

Sometimes it is easy to secure birch bark from fallen trees. Of course, this would make wonderful material for invitations, but a director should of course see that no living trees are skinned.

Headbands may be made by taking two strips of unbleached muslin and stitching them vertically every half inch. Feathers, which may be obtained from a meat market, are slipped into the small openings. They are much prettier when dyed. Bands may be fastened with a safety pin.

Indians would like to follow footprints, either those made by man or wild beast, in the manner described in the Daniel Boone Party (page 121).

Invitations: Brown paper, crayons.

Games: Paper on which to write name, pencils, pins, headbands, feathers, safety pins, bean bags, targets, animal crackers, shelled corn, two bowls for each relay team, beads, needles, thread, small dish for each guest, dishpan tom-tom.

Favors: Indian favors.

Circus Party

PENNY COOKE AND HER LITTLE FRIENDS HAD SEEN A CIRCUS; and ever since that August day they had played among themselves at being clowns, elephants, and bareback riders. In fact, they talked of little else. That was what gave Penny the idea of giving a circus party.

As the clowns were her favorite performers, the young hostess decided that they should bear the twelve invitations to her party. To make each one, she traced the picture of a funny-faced clown holding a circus hoop, colored him with gaudy colors, and wrote the particulars of the invitation inside the hoop.

Penny next turned her attention to place cards, jolly little rocking horses on which clowns might like to ride. To make each one, she cut two identical horses from cardboard, one for each side of her animal. Next she cut a little blanket from brightly colored paper and pasted it across the two backs so that half hung on either side. She separated the rockers by pasting a small cardboard bracket between the bases of the two sides of the horse at their centers. With great care, she pasted the black eyes, reins, and brightly colored trappings in place, thus finishing a little horse that could really rock.

"There they are, Mother, ready for clowns to ride," she said, placing the horses in a straight line at the back of her very own work table.

"What clowns?" asked her mother, only half thinking.

"Why, Beppo Kenneth Hyde, Ricco Alice Brown, Marro Tom Smith. Won't the kids have fun when they know I've given them clown names?" Penny laughed as she wrote the names on the rockers.

Penny knew that she would have to have animals at her circus party; so she thought of two games using them, an animal hunt, and an animal puzzle game. She made her own puzzles by pasting animal pictures from inexpensive books on cardboard and then cutting them into large pieces. Each puzzle had the same number of pieces. In preparation for the hunt, Penny and her mother and daddy spent several evenings cutting elephants, lions, and tigers from construction paper.

"Oh, Mother, you have helped me so much. Can't you come to my party?" asked Penny, as her mother kissed her good night the evening before the great event.

"It's your party, Penny. Would you really like me to come?"

"Oh, yes, indeed," answered the little girl.

"I'll tell you what I'll do," suggested her mother. "I'll dress up in a big clown suit and assist you with some of the games."

The last task before the big event was transforming the front room into a menagerie tent. Penny collected all the stuffed dogs, elephants, monkeys, and other animals that had ever been given to her and placed them about the room so that they peeped from behind chairs, from the mantel, and from the bookcases. She made signs, reading, "Do not feed the elephant"; "Do not tease the monkey"; "Keep your hands away from the cages," and propped them before her specimens.

"I'd really like to feed your elephant," remarked a little boy who arrived before the other guests.

"Nope; it's forbidden," said the hostess. "But here comes someone else. As you've seen the menagerie, suppose you show her around." As the guests viewed the exhibition, they put on a first-class show, imitating the people they had seen at the real circus in the summer.

Soon Penny's mother, the Big Clown, entered the room with sad news.

CIRCUS ANIMAL HUNT

"Although some of the animals are still in the cages, many have been lost. They are little paper animals. Won't you help us find them?" she asked as she gave each child a paper sack which she termed a "cage."

The children proved themselves to be first-class big game hunters as they found the escaped beasts behind the draperies and in all corners and nooks of the room. After five minutes of searching, the Big Clown called her aides together and counted the animals in each "cage" as Penny kept the score. A little girl who found more animals than any of the other guests had found was given a cuddly stuffed elephant.

ANIMAL PUZZLES

"It was so kind of you to help us find our animals," said Penny, "but we are having all kinds of bad luck. Some of the beasts which were not lost have fallen to pieces." She asked the children to sit in a circle on the floor and gave each one an envelope containing one of her home-made puzzles. All hurried to get the broken pieces together. A little boy with clever fingers who finished his first was given a larger, more complicated puzzle for a prize; but all the boys and girls were allowed to finish and were given their puzzles as favors.

CALLIOPE

"Calliope," Penny's name for musical chairs, was the next game on the program. Penny's mother started to play the lively strains of "I went to the animal fair," as Penny and her guests placed chairs side by side alternately facing opposite walls. There was one less chair than children. When everything was ready, the guests lined up next to the chairs and then marched around them. Suddenly the music stopped. Each youngster scrambled for a seat, but a little boy who happened to be at the end of the line was left standing. He removed a chair from the line and sat on it at the side of the room. He wasn't lonesome, for each time the game was repeated he had more company to watch with him. Soon one of the boys was alone in the center. Penny gave him an inexpensive music box as a prize.

BIG SHOW

Penny blew a big whistle announcing that it was time for the big performance to begin. She told her guests that they were about to become

RICCO ALICE BROWN

circus performers and asked them to sit in a large circle on the floor. She whispered into the ear of each the name of some circus personage, the clown, the tight rope walker, the trained dog, the monkey, the seal. One little boy said out loud that he didn't know how to be a seal. Penny beckoned him to come over to the side of the room, requested him to keep his identity a secret, and then asked him to be a pony, showing him how a pony might trot. When all the performers were ready, Penny stood in the center of the circle and in turn pointed to each person to put on his act. Not a word was spoken except in animal language. After each guest finished his act, the children guessed what he represented.

REFRESHMENTS

The show was stopped by summons from the Big Clown to the mess tent, and what a sight it was! A riot of color with inflated balloons tied to each chair! In the center of the table was a big round cake with striped peppermint sticks resting against its sides and animal crackers walking around in the frosting on the top. More animal crackers were strewn all over the table, and the rocking horses marked each place. Even the dinner plates suggested the big top. In each mound of mashed potato was a little pennant flying on a toothpick. Near each mound were creamed chip beef and peas.

The ice cream was served on circus carts with graham-cracker bodies and gumdrop wheels. Each cart was made by placing four round gumdrops on two skewers which served as axles and then laying a double graham cracker on top of that. Of course, they were served on plates, as they were not very substantial. When everything else was served, Penny cut the large circus cake and gave everyone a piece.

SUGGESTIONS

This party is planned for a child about eight years of age; but with more help from a parent, a five-year-old child may give it. A small child might help with the invitations by pasting bright patches of construction paper on the clown's suit. Small children should not be given prizes as here mentioned, and there should be no contest in connection with puzzle making. Any room will serve for the scene of the affair.

Church and school groups may well use these plans if the puzzle game is omitted and the refreshments are made more simple. If there is a large number of children present, it would be well to divide the guests into groups of not more than twenty.

To make pennants, cut a small triangle from brightly colored paper and paste the large side to a toothpick. If there is no construction paper available, the hostess may cut out brightly colored pieces from magazine advertisements to decorate her rocking horses.

FLYING JINNY

If there are not enough chairs to play "calliope," "flying Jinny" may be substituted. To play this there must be an odd number of participants.

They form two concentric circles with the odd child in the center. The child in the center is given a noise maker which he blows as the children in the inner circle move left and those in the outer circle move right. The center child suddenly stops making his noise and takes hold of a child in either circle. As the noise stops, all the other children try to find partners. The child left standing alone becomes the center player. After playing the game two or three times, the two circles change places, as the center player is most likely to choose a partner from the inner circle.

"The clown has lost his donkey," played with the same rules as those in "Bo Peep and her sheep" in the Mother Goose Party (page 96), would fit perfectly into these plans. The clown is blindfolded and calls, "Here, Pete!" as the donkey answers, "He haw."

MATERIALS NEEDED

Invitations: Paper, pencil, crayons.

Decorations: Stuffed animals, signs, balloons, pennants in mashed potatoes, graham-cracker carts with gumdrop wheels and skewer axles.

Games: Construction-paper animals, inexpensive picture books and cardboard for puzzles, paper sack for each guest, chair for all but one guest, musical instrument, whistle.

Favors: Stuffed elephant, music box, construction-paper rocking horses, puzzle.

Farmers' Party

7HIS ATTIC LOOKS LIKE A BARN," SAID NATALIE FRY'S MOTHER one day as she was looking for a bit of tatting in a trunk.

"That's an idea, Mother. Perhaps I can make it look like a barn and give a farmers' party. What do you think of the idea?"

Natalie's mother put her O.K. on the idea at once, with one reservation, that she would do her part in making it look like an attic again once the party was over.

Natalie made her own invitations. On each sheet of paper she drew the pictures of a scarecrow, a pig, and a rooster; and below them she wrote the particulars of the invitation, which included instructions for the guests to come dressed in work clothes.

The attic trunks were quickly pushed to one side of the room and covered with burlap bags, and dried corn was hung from the rafters. Natalie made a scarecrow herself and let it decorate one corner, and from a cousin she borrowed harness to hang in a conspicuous place. She made a big chart which she thought looked like an egg chart, but was really her way of keeping score for her friends' games. On the day of the party, she scattered hay on the floor.

"Well, Hiram, how's your crops?" asked the young hostess of the first arrival.

"Pretty good, pretty good," answered the overall-clad guest quickly falling into the agrarian swing of things. "But I sure am mightily worried about my brindle calf."

"Excuse my looks," interrupted a young girl, "but I had this apron on to cook dinner for the hired man, and I forgot to change before I came over. If I take it off now, I'm afraid I'll leave it somewhere."

Fortunately there were no real farmers present, or they would have had one big laugh at their city cousins' lack of information on farm affairs; but the boys and girls talked glibly just like the farmers they had read about in the funny papers or seen in the movies.

PITCHING

"Now boys, and womenfolk too," remarked Natalie, "I want to see how good your pitching is. There are two things which will count, speed and accuracy." She divided the guests into relay teams and gave each person five kernels of corn. In front of each team she placed a pan. At a signal, the leaders tried to pitch their corn into the pan. Natalie ruled that only one kernel might be thrown at a time. As soon as a leader tossed the last kernel, he stepped aside and went to the end of the line, and the guest behind him began to throw. Each person tossed his corn and Natalie scored two sets of points on the chart, one point for each member of the team which had the greatest number in its pan, and one point for each member of the team which finished first.

Natalie gave five more kernels of corn to each guest and this time counted only accuracy.

COCK A DOODLE DOO

"Cock a doodle doo! My dame has lost her shoe," crowed an aide of Natalie over in the corner.

"You hear that?" asked the hostess. "Better do something about it." She divided the guests into two groups and asked one group to stand in a far corner of the room. She requested the other guests to be seated on chairs placed in a straight line and to remove their left shoes. Quickly she picked up the shoes and piled them in the center of the room. When she gave the signal, the first group of guests left its corner; and each picked up a shoe, hunted for the owner, and put it on him. The person first to get a shoe on the correct foot received five points on the chart; the second, four; the third, three; the fourth, two; and the fifth, one. The sides changed

COME BACK TO THE FARM
DRESS LIKE A FARMER
ACT LIKE A FARMER
SEPT. 23, 4 O'CLOCK
NATALIE FRY
218 W. BLANK ST.   PLEASE REPLY

places, and scores were again given to the five guests who first put on the correct shoes.

NEEDLE RELAY

"I know your hands are rough from doing outside work," the hostess told her guests, "but I want you to keep them agile just the same." She divided the guests into two relay teams and had them line up so that each guest had a partner. To one contestant of each leading pair she gave a large-eyed darning needle and to the other a piece of linen thread. At a signal, the four leaders ran to a designated spot. One of each pair held the needle in his hand as the other endeavored to put the thread through the eye without touching his hands to the steel. With the thread safely in the needle, the pair ran back to their team and gave the thread and needle to the next ones in line to repeat the action. The young farmers were so excited and laughed so hard that they truly did have difficulty in executing their stunt, but each one at last did his part. Natalie gave a score to each member of the team which finished first. Then she suggested that the partners change about, so that those who had previously held the needle did the threading. Much to the surprise of everyone, the other team won.

GOING TO TOWN

"It's Saturday night," announced Natalie. "You'd better get dressed ready to go to town." She lined the guests into relay teams again and gave each leader a suitcase containing an old hat, a discarded coat, a large pair of gloves, and a pair of her father's rubbers. At a signal, each leader ran to the opposite wall, put on all the clothes, closed the case, "slushed" back to his team as quickly as he could and still keep the rubbers on his feet, took off the extra garments, put them in the case, shut it, and gave it to the next person in line to repeat the action. Every farmer had his opportunity to go to town, but more than one lost his rubbers in his hurry and had to stop to put them on again. Nobody really cared who won this race, but Natalie gave a point to each member of the team which finished first.

BRINGING IN STOCK

"It's getting rather late," opined Natalie. "I guess we better get the stock in for the night. She gave each guest a slip of paper on which was written the name of an animal. There was an equal number of cows, pigs, dogs, and cats. At her signal, the guests started to circulate around the room each making the noise of the animal he represented. The cows mooed, the pigs grunted, the dogs barked, and the cats mewed. When two dogs found each other, they joined hands and continued to look for other dogs. All the other animals did likewise. At the end of two minutes, Natalie blew a whistle. She gave a point to each member of the team which had the largest number of animals together.

One glance at the chart told Natalie that a red-haired boy had the highest score. She gave him a big straw hat. A little girl who had the second highest score received a big red handkerchief.

REFRESHMENTS

A clanging dinner bell, changed Natalie's mind about playing another game. Down in the dining room the guests went, where they found the table covered with a red and white checked paper tablecloth and centered with a big bouquet of carrots and celery. Big red apples on which place cards were pinned marked each place. The menu was enough for any farmer: potato salad with lots of vegetables in it, milk, weenies, and great big homemade cookies.

SUGGESTIONS

Boys and girls from eight to thirteen years of age may give this party with almost no help. As there are a number of relay races in the plans, almost any number of guests may be invited. For this reason school and church groups will find these plans helpful.

If there are only eight or ten guests, the host may wish to change "cock a doodle doo" a little. Each guest must sacrifice one shoe, which the host puts in a pile in the center of the room. At a signal, the guests rush for the pile, select their own shoes, and return to the side of the room where they put them on.

POTATO RELAY

If the party is very small, a potato relay may be substituted for the threading-the-needle contest. The host divides the guests into two relay teams, gives each leader a big spoon, and places a dish of potatoes in front of each line. At a signal, each leader balances a potato on his spoon, carries it across the room, deposits it, and returns, giving the spoon to the next in line.

THE FARMER SAYS

If the party must be given in a rather small room, the animal matching game may not be practical. In its place, the guests may play "the farmer says." The host stands before his guests and moves his arms in some direction saying, "The farmer says do this." The guests copy his movements until the host says, "His wife says do this." Anyone who follows the movement then drops out of the game. The faster the leader moves and talks, the more guests he will catch making false moves. The game continues until only one person is left following the leader.

Many an old farmhouse did not have lights. Blowing out the candle as described in the Frontier Party (page 150) might be played.

MATERIALS NEEDED

Invitations: Paper, pencil or pen and India ink, crayons or water colors.

Decorations: Burlap bags, farm equipment, scarecrow, hay, dried corn, vegetable bouquet, red and white table spread.

Games: Egg chart on which to keep a record of points won in games, ten kernels of corn for each guest, dish for each relay team, chairs for half of the guests, needle and thread for each relay team, suitcase for each relay team containing hat, coat, pair of gloves, and pair of rubbers, slips of paper on which are names of animals, whistle, dinner bell.

Favors: Red handkerchief, straw hat.

120

Daniel Boone Party

PAPER MEN, DRESSED EXACTLY LIKE THE FORMER FRONTIER scouts with leather jackets and fur caps, summoned the guests to the Daniel Boone party which William George gave at his home. After tracing the pictures of the scouts, Will wrote the particulars of the invitation on pieces of brown paper cut to resemble the small animal skins which pioneers often used to bind agreements or keep records and tucked them under his messengers' belts.

Turning the recreation room into an old-time fort was an easy job. Will covered the lights with paper lanterns, and hung brown paper over the windows to represent the skins the pioneers used in place of glass. The only chairs were straight-backed ones. To give a woodsy odor he placed pine boughs about the room.

Since Will knew that all scouts had to have powder horns, he made one out of heavy brown paper for each guest. They were only pictures, shaped like the one which the scout messenger wore; but he cut them out and tied strings through the small ends so that the guests could tie them around their waists. Then he made many pine-tree stickers. He secured heavy brown gummed tape, drew the pictures of trees, cut them out, and colored them green.

As the guests arrived, Will gave each his powder horn, explaining that during the course of the afternoon it would become decorated with small pine trees.

FOOTPRINT RELAY

"The Indians attacked this fort, Boonesborough, last night and then retreated," Will told his hardy scouts. "During the course of the afternoon, we are going to find them if we can. Now our first job will be to follow their footprints across the open field."

He divided the scouts into two groups and directed them to line up in relay teams. Each leader was given two large footprints cut from brown paper. At the beginning of the race, he was directed to place both feet on one print. At a signal, he placed the other print in front of him, put both feet on that, and then placed the first print in front, stepping on that. In this manner he proceeded across the room, touched the opposite wall, and returned to his team in the same manner. He gave the prints to the next in line to repeat the action. The second man on one team put one print so far ahead of the place where he was standing that he lost his balance and let one foot touch the floor. He had to go back to his team and start again. The race continued until each scout finished his trek across the open field following the prints. Will gave pine-tree stickers to the scouts of the team which finished first. The stickers were pasted to the horns.

BUFFALO PATH RELAY

"Now that you are at the edge of the forest, you must follow the buffalo path through the woods," explained the young host as he twisted strings of equal length around the room. He gave the leader of each group of scouts a field glass and asked him to look through it backward so that his feet seemed very, very far away. The leaders were directed to start following the strings without taking their eyes off the glass. Will ruled that if anyone got both feet off the string, he had to start again. It all sounded very easy, but the leaders soon began to wobble a little as they walked. Once at the end of the string they ran back to their teams via the shortest route and the next scouts started out. Soon all the scouts had followed the path, and Will again awarded stickers to the team members who finished first.

INDIAN HUNT

"The Indian chief is hiding in ambush," Will whispered. "You are all to look for him. When someone is near, the war drum will beat loudly.

When no one is around him, it will beat softly." The chief was a little doll, and the war drum was a tin pan which Will beat with a potato masher The scouts began to look high and low, and soon one spied the doll in a corner behind a chair. He was given two seals.

INDIAN FIGHT

"Here are Indians ready to fight," said Will as he placed three milk bottles about six feet from each spot which he designated as a starting place for each team. He asked the men again to line up in relay teams behind the starting spots and gave each leader three marbles. According to the host's direction, the leaders rolled the marbles trying to hit the bottles in front of their teams. One leader hit the same bottle twice, but only one of those shots was counted. As Will recorded the score of each, the leaders picked up the marbles and gave them to the next scouts in line, who tried to hit the Indians. Each scout was given an opportunity to "shoot," and the stickers were awarded to team members having the highest total team score.

ENEMY'S CAMP

"I am sorry to tell you that you have all been taken prisoners by other Indians while you were fighting these few in front of you," said Will. "But now that you are in the enemy's camp, I want you to take careful note of all that you see so that you can draw a map for the people at the fort."

Will showed them a table where a camp with little paper figures of Indians, campfires, trees, bows, arrows, streams, and canoes was all set out. He asked them to make mental notes of the things which they saw and the positions. After five minutes, he gave each scout a pencil with an eraser and a piece of paper and asked them first to list all the articles which they had seen, placing a number before each name. Then he asked them to draw little maps putting numbers in the positions of the articles. For instance, one list began: (1) Indian man, (2) wigwam, (3) stream." As the wigwam stood over on the left-hand side of the setting, the scout put a "2" on the left-hand side of his paper. The wigwam stood next to the stream; so he put

DANIEL
BOONE
PARTY
OCT. 4
4 O'CLOCK
WILLIAM
GEORGE
315 PROSPECT
PLEASE REPLY

a "3" near that. Near the wigwam stood an Indian brave; so a "1" was placed near the "2."

Will didn't tell anyone where anything stood, but he did help them individually so that each person understood how to draw the map. The scouts accepted the challenge and really concentrated on map making. Of course, no one had everything correct, but Will gave a sticker to each person who had some part of the map as it was on the setting. In addition, he gave five stickers to a lad who listed all the articles correctly, and then gave four to the one who had the nearest number correct, three to the next, two to the fourth, and one to the fifth.

ESCAPE RELAY

"Really your maps were wonderful," said the leader. "Fortunately, you are going to be able to escape so that they may be of some value to the people at the fort. Of course, the Indians wouldn't let you just walk away. They have tied you up." He requested the scouts to form relay teams again and gave each one a cord to tie around his ankles. At a signal, the leaders hopped across the room and back again, touching the next person in line, who did the same thing. When each scout had made his escape, Will gave a sticker to the members of the team which finished first.

Safe home at last, the scouts wrote their names on their horns and gave them to Will, who counted the stickers. He gave a jackknife to a boy who had the largest number of stickers and a book on woodcraft to a girl who had the second largest number.

REFRESHMENTS

"Well, scouts," said Will, "I guess after all those adventures you must be ready to eat almost anything. Just help me put these plates on this table, and I'll see what I can find for you in the line of grub." As the guests pulled up the chairs and put the plates at each place, Will brought in a big steaming dish of scalloped corn, and a plate piled high with fresh biscuits. He later served ice cream.

As the scouts were diving into the biscuits, and spreading them with butter and honey, Will said, "Let's tell some of our most exciting escapes from the Indians. Grandpa told me one about Boone that is supposed to be true. He was on the rafters of a shed outside the fort drying some tobacco when he looked below him and saw four Indians pointing guns at him.

" 'Boone no escape this time,' they said.

"Boone welcomed them, joked with them, and promised to be their prisoner if they would let him finish his work. He descended from the rafters and picked up a handful of dried tobacco. When the Indians looked aside, he threw an armful into their faces; and while they were choking and sneezing, he ran to the fort."

Then the guests started to make up tales about their adventures. Each story grew longer until Will was very, very sure that it was just too bad to think that Uncle Sam no longer had need of scouts who could do that particular kind of brave deed.

SUGGESTIONS

Boys and girls from about seven years of age to fourteen may give this party. It is particularly fitted to the needs of clubs and classes looking for novel group entertainment. If the children are quite young, it might be well just to name the articles seen in the Indian camp. Older children, however, with very little guidance may make good maps.

Making the camp may take several afternoons. Little pictures may be drawn on rough paper and cut out and colored. Classes or clubs may enjoy doing this in advance. Another idea would be to have each guest draw at the party and cut out a picture of an Indian, a tree, a wigwam, and other articles. Then the host might place them on the table in any manner he wished. The test would then be only remembering positions.

A young host also might prefer to send the animal skin only for an invitation rather than attempt the more complicated drawing of the scout.

When the Indian warfare is over, the scouts might like to go hunting as described in the Cowboy Party (page 61).

Invitations: Paper, pencil or pen and India ink, crayons or water colors.

Decorations: Brown paper to cover windows, paper lanterns, pine boughs.

Games: Paper powder horns, pine trees of heavy sticky paper painted green (around Christmas time it is easy to get pine-tree stickers), two brown paper footprints for each relay team, long string for each relay team, field glass for each team, little Indian chief doll, tin pan and potato masher tom-tom, three milk bottles for each team, three marbles for each team, Indian camp with paper figures, pencil and paper for each guest, cord for each guest.

Favors: Jackknife, book on woodcraft.

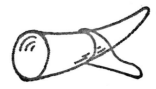

Halloween Party

$\mathcal{A}$s THE FOUR WINDS HOWLED AND THE EERIE SPIRITS BEGAN TO practice their midnight walks in preparation for the night of all saints, Bob Blakesly designed the invitations for his Halloween party. He traced a picture of a bony ghost and a wicked witch dancing around a big black cauldron from which a misty smoke emerged and circled around the details of the invitation, and copied it on pieces of orange paper.

Bob made his residence look like the home of a witch and a ghost. He lighted it with yellow and black tapers in old bottles and glaring jack-o'-lanterns. On the curtains he pinned big black bats and cats made of construction paper. Down in the recreation room, he strung some clothesline taut and from it suspended bright red apples on strings. All around this room he hid small owls, cats, and bats made of construction paper.

His father and his mother agreed to aid him at the beginning of the party by donning sheets and becoming ghosts with him. As the pirates, babies, hoboes, Spanish dancing girls, gypsy men, and all the other queer guests who were invited began to arrive, Bob stationed himself at the door to greet them in ghostlike manner. With stealthy motions, Bob's mother beckoned them upstairs, and his father, who wore wet rubber gloves, shook hands with them and pointed to the bedroom. When the wraps were removed, his mother again took the guests in hand and beckoned them to advance to the recreation room, which was considerably lighter than the other rooms.

RECOGNIZING GHOSTS

Soon Bob joined his guests and in a monotone said, "My friends, you think you know who you are, but you are mistaken. You are really the reincarna-

129

tion of some great spirits whom you think dead. On each of your backs, I shall pin the name of the person you really are. By asking questions which may be answered by yes and no, you may discover your identity. You may ask only one question of any guest at a time. If you ask a question and he answers it, you in turn must answer his. Do not ask if you are a specific person until you are quite sure you know the right name, for you may have only two incorrect guesses." Bob pinned the names of the people whom everybody knew on the backs of the guests. His list included George Washington, Abraham Lincoln, Betsy Ross—all people about whom his friends had studied in school.

The boys and girls started out asking general questions, such as, "Am I a man? Am I an American? Did I live during the Civil War? Was I ever president of the United States? Was I a writer? Did I write plays?" At last each came to some specific question, such as "Did I make the first American Flag?" or "Did I chop down a cherry tree?" after which the direct question, "Am I Betsy Ross?" or, "Am I George Washington?" was asked. The game continued until each person guessed his identity.

"You are great, you are noble," continued the ghostlike Bob. "May the spirit of the men who made the path easier for you never die. To you who best remembered who he was, I give this prize to light your path through life," he intoned, handing a funny little paper pumpkin jack-o'-lantern with candle inside to the boy who first guessed his identity.

APPLE BOBBING

Breaking into a more lively mood, Bob told his guests that the apples suspended from the ceiling were not just for decoration. He asked each person to stand before one with his hands behind his back and try to eat the fruit. There was bobbing of a new order as the apples swung back and forth as they were touched. Somehow or other, most of the boys and girls were able to get their first bites, after which the rest was easy eating. Of course, each guest was given his apple, and a candy apple was awarded to a young pirate who took the first real bite.

130

"The cats, owls, and bats are all out tonight," Bob chanted, again assuming the eerie voice. "They are hidden all around the room. To him who finds the most, a prize shall be given."

Bob allowed his guests only five minutes for the hunt, during which time they looked high and low for the little construction-paper figures. Bob gave a little stuffed black cat to a Colonial lady who had a large collection.

RETURNED GHOSTS

"You are all very much alive today," said the ghost host, "but some day you too will be ghosts. Please do as I direct so that you may have practice in haunting your friends." He divided the guests into two groups, asking one section to leave the room and the other to be seated on the floor as he passed around pencils and paper. He turned off all but one small light.

Soon a departed guest, now draped like a ghost, returned.

"He will answer three questions," explained Bob, "and you must then guess his identity."

"How do you like being a ghost?" asked one boy.

"You will learn for yourself some-day," replied the ghost in an eerie voice.

"What do ghosts eat?" was the next question.

"Next to nothing," said the ghost.

"What's your name?" asked some-one, just for fun.

"That's for you to guess," answered the visitor as he left the room.

Each departed guest was a ghost; then the teams changed places. Bob gave two prizes of candied apples; one to the guest who guessed the most names correctly, and one to the guest who disguised his voice the best.

MAGIC CARPET

"Tonight is the night of magic," said Bob, "and I have here a magic carpet which I am placing on the floor. It is charmed so that whoever stands on it when there is no music is out of luck."

According to his directions, the children marched across the carpet and around its end as music was played. No one was allowed to jump across it. Suddenly the music stopped. Everyone who had even so much as a toe touching the magic cloth when the music stopped was asked to withdraw from the game. Round and round the children marched until at last there were only two playing. Bob gave them each a jack-o'-lantern.

FORTUNES

Bob had his own way of telling fortunes. He placed on the floor a large cardboard which was divided into squares, each bearing a number. He asked his guests to line up and gave each one a bean. The first guest tossed his bean on square 6 on the board. Bob drew number 6 fortune from a box and gave it to his guest to read aloud, "Be careful next winter not to slip on ice. You will hurt your dignity if you do."

One by one the guests tossed the beans, each receiving news of a humorous fate. Bob tossed his bean at the end of the game. His fortune was marked with a "50" so that he could draw it regardless of the showing on the board. It said, "Beware! Your friends may turn against you if you do not feed them. The ghost and the witch request their presence at dinner."

REFRESHMENTS

Into the dining room, dimly lighted with jack-o'-lanterns, Bob led his guests. All around the room were paper owls, bats, and cats. In the center of the table was a spooky graveyard with marshmallow tombstones over which pipestem-cleaner men were climbing. Above it was suspended a yellow half-moon. An ugly witch marked each place.

The menu consisted of witch's salad (fruit with big black dates), witch's brew (hot chocolate), ghost sandwiches (cream cheese on white bread), and ghost ice cream (plain vanilla).

SUGGESTIONS

This party is planned for children about twelve years of age. By making the guessing of names a little easier, children as young as eight years may give it. Rather than using the names of deceased people, the host may pin the names of types of workers on the guests' backs. The questions may then be: "Do I work with my hands? Do I use a typewriter when I work? Do I use a needle when I work? Do I work indoors?" The host may give point to the game by saying, "You here gathered are pirates, dancers, tramps; the ghosts of your ancestors are still with you. They followed other trades. I shall pin the name of each on your back and you must guess what it is." He will then give explanations similar to those in the story.

As the games in this plan may be played by large and small groups, church and school classes may give it.

FROG RELAY

If the party is large, a frog relay may be substituted for the hunt for construction-paper figures. The boys and girls are divided into relay teams, and each leader is given a burlap bag. At a signal, he must get into the bag, hop across the room and back again, get out of the bag, and give it to his teammate behind him, who does the same thing. Each guest must have a chance to hop, but the team whose members finish first of course win the contest.

In place of the apple bobbing contest, the host might have a pumpkin grabbing contest, fashioned like the "anchor pulling" contest in the Skipper Party (page 93). Candy pumpkins are tied to the ends of strings.

133

Invitations: Paper, pen and India ink, or pencil.

Decorations: Jack-o'-lanterns, candles in bottles, big black bats, cats, owls of construction paper, witch place cards, paper moon, marshmallow gravestones, pipestem-cleaner figures.

Games: Little cats, owls, bats made of constuction paper, apples on strings tied to rope strung taut across recreation room, sheets for assistant ghosts, wet gloves, name of deceased person written on sheet of paper for each guest, pins, pencil and paper for each guest, carpet, music, cardboard divided into squares bearing numbers, fortune for each number, beans.

Favors: Three candy apples, stuffed cat, jack-o'-lanterns.

Pirate Party

THE SIGN OF THE SKULL, THE MARK OF ALL PIRATES INCLUDING the great Captain Kidd, John Silver, Kingston, and Ballantyne, summoned guests to the pirate party which John Smith gave in the basement of his home. To create this eerie invitation, John traced the outline on a double sheet of paper so that the top of the skull came on a fold, cut out the eyes and nose on the top sheet, and colored them red on the under sheet.

He soon transformed the basement of his home into the dreary cabins of a pirate ship. Old boxes and chests made excellent furniture; and by trimming large pieces of cardboard the size of the windows and cutting a large circle in each, he made portholes. The most of the light came from candles which he placed in tin cans and fastened to the walls where they could not be tipped over.

PIRATE MAKE-UP

When the guests arrived, John professed to be astonished at their civilized appearance, but soon showed them a remedy for it. He escorted them to one corner of the basement where there was a pile of inexpensive brightly colored material which was cut into sashes and bandanas. On a box near by were cold cream, grease paint, plaster, and large earrings made from brass curtain rings with strings attached. Above it hung an old mirror. With wild whoops, the boys and girls began to transform themselves into the boldest men who ever sailed the seven seas. Some elected to give themselves putty noses, others tied black patches over one eye, and still others painted the most dreadful gashes on their faces with brilliant lipstick. They tied bandanas around their heads, slipped the strings of the earrings over their ears, and fastened sashes around their waists. At John's request,

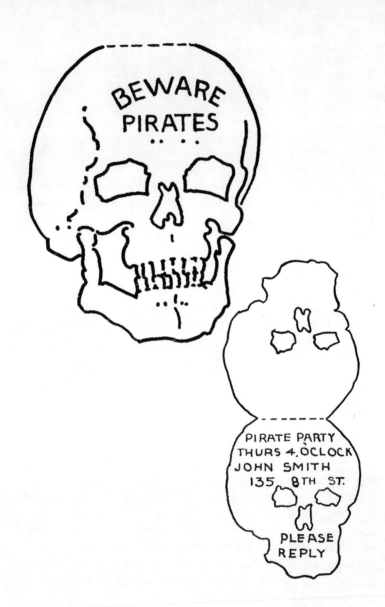

each chose a new name, a name only a pirate should have, like "Terrible Tim" and "Half Pint Joe," wrote it on a slip of paper, and pinned it to his garments so that all the world might address him in pirate fashion.

SHADOW PIRATES

As the bold men of the seas swaggered about, John asked them to determine to which crew they would belong. He passed around a wooden bowl in which were slips of paper with the names, "Ship of Bones" and "Ship of Skulls," written on them. He explained that pirates just had to have information about each other's crews and that sometimes they had to make their decisions when vision was blurred by distance, fog, or twilight. Guessing shadow pirates, he pointed out, would give them good practice. Hanging a sheet in the center of the room, he asked the members of the crew of the "Ship of Bones" to sit on boxes on one side of it and gave each one a sheet of paper and a pencil. He placed a lamp on the other side of the sheet and requested the crew of the "Ship of Skulls" to gather over there.

"Pirates came from all walks of life, you know," he explained "and often they tried to hide their identity by assuming a hunch back or queer ways of walking." He directed a member of the crew of the "Ship of Skulls" to walk past the sheet casting a good profile shadow. The members of the other crew guessed at the identity and wrote down the real name and the assumed. One by one the pirates paraded until each had a turn. Then the two crews changed places, and the crew of the "Ship of Skulls" endeavored to identify the members of the crew of the "Ship of Bones." John gave three prizes, one to a boy who had the most real names correctly identified with the shadows, one to a girl who paired the most chosen names with the real names correctly, and one to a boy whose shadow only a few people identified.

TREASURE IDENTIFICATION

"I want you people to find out what treasure there is in the other room," John told his guests. He gave each one a pencil and paper and took them to

137

a table where a great assortment of inexpensive necklaces, bracelets, coins, and trinkets was set out. He let them look at the loot for five minutes and then asked each one to write down all that he could remember.

WALKING THE PLANK

As each one finished writing, he was led to another room where Terrible Captain John and an assistant explained to him that his account was so bad that he would have to walk the plank. But, they continued, if he walked just to the end and no further, and if he did not step to either side, he would be spared the fate of falling into the briny deep. On the floor was a strip of white cheesecloth a foot wide and five feet long. John blindfolded the guest and turned him around three times, talking to him all the time, asking him if he could see, and reminding him of the importance of each step. In the meantime, the partner quietly rolled up the "plank." With great care, the blindfolded pirate measured each step until he thought he had reached the end of the "plank." He was then unblindfolded, and was of course embarrassed to learn that he had been fooled. But he had the fun of seeing the next pirate being fooled in the same way.

After each pirate had walked the plank, John admitted that after all there were good descriptions of the loot and gave a prize for the best list.

HIDDEN TREASURE

The time came at last to hunt for the treasure. John explained that in the room a small coin was hidden, of all things, in plain sight. He asked the pirates to look for it and when a person found it to sit down and not say a word, but wait until all were seated. The boys and girls began to look. At last one lad saw the coin on a small bench. Rather than sit down there, he crossed the room and sat down near the door. Immediately all the children gathered around him and looked all over until at last a girl wandered away from the others, saw the coin, and crossed the room sitting near a table. The remaining pirates knew that the coin couldn't be near both of those pirates who were so widely separated and continued their search around the room. Before long all the guests were on the floor. The boy who first saw the coin had the privilege of hiding it. As it was growing late in the afternoon, John stopped the game after four times.

REFRESHMENTS

In a jiffy he solicited the assistance of his guests and set rough boards across sawhorses for a long table. The boxes were pulled up for chairs and the guests gathered around as John helped his mother serve hot soup and biscuits and later ice cream.

PIRATE TALES

"How did you happen to become a pirate, Peg-leg?" the host asked a talkative friend.

"It's a long story, but I'll make it short," said Peg-leg thinking quickly. "I was caught in a windstorm when I was fishing, blown right off my boat, miles and miles through the air, and I landed on a pirate ship. What could I do but be a pirate?"

"I did better than that," said one called Dagger Joe. "I was inspecting ships in the harbor when one set sail while I was aboard. It was a pirate ship. The men on it were such good fun that I thought I'd be a pirate and stop worrying."

Each tale grew a little longer and funnier as each guest explained how he became a pirate. Long before they finished, John served the ice cream. When the stories were ended, the young host said, "Well lads, you have been looking for gold for a long time. Here is a pot of it."

He placed a big dish covered with yellow crepe paper in the center of the table. From it emerged strings which he gave to the guests. At his signal they all pulled, and out came rubber daggers and popguns.

SUGGESTIONS

Boys and girls from eight to fourteen years of age find great fun in acting pirates. The size of the rooms where the party may be given will largely determine the number of guests that may be entertained. About ten might be invited to a home and twenty-five to an affair given by a church or school group in a hall. More may be entertained if the groups are divided for the shadow pictures and the walking the plank contests.

SHIP'S CARGO

If there is time the guests may tell what was in their loaded ships. The first may say, "I sailed the seven seas, and in my ship I had a chest." The second man repeats what has been said and adds an article. Each in turn repeats all the articles and adds one more. When a person gets one article out of order or forgets one, he withdraws from the game. The person to remember the most articles wins the contest.

If there is still time for another game, the guests may have a "dressing to go into port" relay fashioned like the "going to town" relay in the Farmers' Party (page 118).

MATERIALS NEEDED

Invitations: Paper, red crayons, and pencil.

Decorations: Old boxes, chests, cardboard for windows, candles in tin cans, sawhorses, planks.

Games: Inexpensive sashes and bandanas, make-up materials, curtain rings with strings attached for earrings, pencils and slips of paper on which to write chosen names, pins, wooden bowl, slips of paper with "Ship of Bones" and "Ship of Skulls" written on them, sheet, lamp, paper and pencil for each guest, table on which is placed an assortment of bracelets, necklaces, trinkets, cheesecloth five feet long and one foot wide, coin, handkerchief for blindfold, and dish covered with yellow crepe paper.

Favors: Rubber daggers, popguns, and four prizes. If the guests are young, they will enjoy receiving little sailboats. If they are older, they will have just as much fun receiving an honor like a paper skull and crossbones pinned to their bandanas.

140

Doll Party

"WILL YOU AND YOUR DOLLY COME TO MY PARTY?" SO STARTED the little notes which Jane Clark slipped into the pockets of the paper dolls which she made for her friends. Each little doll wore a dear little school dress which Jane colored with her favorite bright crayons. The pockets were only drawn and had a slit across the top into which the note fitted.

Each little girl arrived with her favorite child; for, unlike grown-up mothers, little girls do have chosen babies. Jane took the little guests up to her room, suggesting that they lay their coats and hats on her bed and place the wraps of the dollies on the miniature bed next to hers.

"Is this Susan?" asked Jane of one of her friends as she examined her doll with bright yellow curls.

"Oh, no," answered the friend, "this is Polly. Susan has a very bad cold. So many children have colds these days. I do hope the other children don't catch hers."

Jane's mother stopped in the doorway listening to the conversation.

"Yes," she said to herself, "I thought I saw Patsy standing in the next room when Mrs. Parker and I were talking this afternoon."

In a very serious manner, the little mothers continued to discuss their children until at last Jane's mother suggested that perhaps the dollies might like to watch their mothers play some games. As that sounded like a great idea to the little girls, they scampered downstairs and placed their darlings on the davenport in the living room.

I SENT A DOLLY

"You all know how to play 'a tisket, a tasket,'" said Jane's mother. "This game is played just the same way, only we are going to use a poor little

141

rag doll for the handkerchief and change the words just a little bit. The song will go:

> 'A tisket, a tasket,
> A green and yellow basket.
> I sent a dolly to my love,
> And on the way I dropped it.
> I dropped it once. I dropped it twice.
> I dropped it three times over.' "

All but one little girl formed a circle. The lone child was given a rag doll and walked around the other guests as they sang the familiar chant. When the place in the song, "I dropped it," was reached, the little girl placed the doll behind a friend and ran as fast as she could. The second little girl gave chase, but was unable to tag her friend before she rounded the circle and darted into the vacant place. The second little girl walked around, dropping the doll when the correct time was reached. As she ran around the circle, she was tagged, and so dropped the doll again. Soon everyone had a chance to run; and as everyone was just a little tired of singing, Jane suggested that they play "toyshop."

TOYSHOP

She placed chairs in a circle and asked her friends to sit in them. Then she gave each one the name of some toy. There were French doll, top, tin soldier, drum, horn, and Teddy bear. Jane was jack-in-the-box. She explained that as she told a story, the other guests must jump up whenever their new names were mentioned and act their part. The word "toyshop" was a signal for all to change chairs, and the girl left standing had to continue the story.

Jane stood in the center of the circle and started her tale: "Once there was a little girl, a very rich little girl who had no toys. She didn't have a French doll"— the French doll stood up and bowed stiffly—"she didn't own a top" —the top turned around—"she didn't have a Teddy bear"—Teddy bear rose and let out a little squeak—"nor did she have a horn, drum, nor tin soldier"

—horn went "toot"; drum said "rat-a-tat"; and tin soldier jumped up and saluted.

" 'You can't have a doll, nor a soldier, nor a top, nor a Teddy bear,' said the little girl's mother, 'for you might break them,' " Jane continued, as her guests popped up in fast succession. " 'You may make too much noise with a drum and a horn' "—drum and horn were quick to act their parts—"So the little girl was very sad and wandered down to the toyshop."

All guests jumped up to change chairs as Jane slid into one, leaving drum standing alone.

Drum was hardly thinking as she started her portion, "In the toyshop"—there was a rapid change.

Of course, the story didn't amount to much; but there were quick changes, and before long everyone was out of breath.

PAPER-SACK DOLLS

"Perhaps the children might like playmates," suggested Jane. "Paper-sack dolls are very easy to make." She put some newspapers on the floor and asked her friends to gather around them as she placed white paper sacks (three inches by five inches), crayons, paste, cotton, crepe paper, yarn, scissors, and string in their midst. The dolls were easily made by drawing faces with crayons at the top of the sacks, stuffing the head portion with cotton, and tying a string at the neckline. Some of the guests made hair by pasting strips of crepe paper in place, and others made little crepe paper hats and attached bits of yarn at the rims to make hair. The gowns were spectacular with strips of paper pasted on them. The paper-sack dolls could be made to stand and looked very grand when placed near the other doll children.

DID YOU EVER SEE A DOLLY?

The guests helped pick up every scrap of paper and cheered when Jane suggested that they play, "Did you ever see a dolly go this way and that?"

The children formed a circle around a chosen leader. They all joined in singing:

"Did you ever see a dolly go this way and that?
      Go this way and that way?
      Go this way and that way?
   Did you ever see a dolly go this way and that?"

As the children sang, the leader made motions with her arms, and the others copied her. At the end of the song, she chose a successor, who elected to raise her knees in time to the chant. Singing was a little hard when one little girl thought that she wanted the others to bend forward and straighten, but somehow or other they managed. Each little girl had an opportunity to be in the center.

BECOMING DOLLS

Suddenly Jane asked, "What kind of doll would you like to be?" She brought out a box of bonnets, skirts, dresses, shoes, everything in that wonderful trunk her mother kept for her. One little girl donned a night-gown and a baby bonnet to be a baby doll. A short skirt and strings of beads attracted the child who wished to be a flapper doll. One child couldn't decide just what she thought she wanted; so she mixed all sorts of garments to be the doll of the ages. As Jane's mother played "The Wedding of the Painted Doll" on the piano, each little mother picked up her child, and together they paraded up to Jane's room, down again, round and round the living room, and at last into the dining room.

REFRESHMENTS

There were more and more dolls. A big boudoir doll was propped up in the center of the table for a centerpiece. Out from her skirts extended ribbons with penny dolls tied to each. Place cards were paper dolls like the invitations with the children's names written at their bases.

In one corner of the room, a little table was set with doll dishes. Jane didn't have doll chairs enough to give one to each guest; so she placed pillows on the floor, and the little mothers agreed that their children looked quite happy sitting there.

WILL YOU
AND YOUR
DOLLY COME
TO MY PARTY
NOV. 18
3 O'CLOCK
JANE CLARK
180 S. PARK AVE
PLEASE REPLY

After their children were settled and happy, the little mothers gathered around the big table for a supper of creamed veal, peas, brown bread, hot chocolate, ice cream, and little cakes that looked like dolls. The cake dough had been baked in crinkly cups which when removed made the edges of the cake look like pleated skirts. In the top of each, Jane's mother put a penny doll so that only the portion of her body above the waist showed.

When the little guests went to say goodbye, they could not help remarking about the number of playmates which the older children had gained during the afternoon. There were the paper dolls, the paper-bag dolls, and the penny dolls.

SUGGESTIONS

Little girls from six to eight years of age will like this party. If they seem to be enjoying themselves very much with any one game, there is no reason to crowd in all these activities. Time should be left for children to dress up, however, for this is considered by many the best known sport.

Parties for little girls, like this one, in the home should be kept small. There is no reason why a Sunday school class or school group of fifteen members could not give it in a larger social hall.

The little girls might also like to string beads for their children.

MATERIALS NEEDED

Invitations: Paper, pencil, scissors, crayons.

Games: Rag doll, chair for all but one child present, newspapers, white bags five by three inches, yarn, scissors, paste, crayons, crepe paper, string, cotton, old clothes.

Decorations: Boudoir doll, penny dolls, ribbons.

Frontier Party

THE OLD COVERED WAGONS PULLED BY STURDY HORSES CARRIED many a family across the vast country. The little paper ones which Ginger Huston drew had a much lighter errand. They merely bore the invitations to a frontier party which Ginger gave at her home. To make these Ginger drew the picture of the rear of a wagon and across the box portion wrote the particulars of the invitation.

Since she knew that these early settlers had very little furniture, she removed all the end tables and lamps from the living room where the party was to be given, making it look as bare as possible. Into this rugged atmosphere came her friends dressed as strong miners, hardy pioneer women, city slickers who went West to get rich quickly, and professional entertainers.

GETTING ACQUAINTED

"I want you folks to get well acquainted," said the hostess, "for out here in the West everyone is a bit more friendly. I know a lot of you are called names other than the ones you were baptized with. Now, you over there, I bet your friends call you 'Happy Pete.' And you're 'Singing Joe.' Now I want each of you to choose a name for yourself and then go about asking everybody else his real name and his nickname. Of course, you must tell people yours too. Just write them all down so you can remember them."

Ginger passed out slips of paper and pencils, and the guests began to move about quickly, scribbling away.

"I guess I have them all," said a boy.

"All right, bring them here," said Ginger. "But the rest of you keep right on writing." As soon as everyone had a complete list, Ginger announced that this boy might be the first governor of the new state.

FRONTIER PARTY

DEC. 15, 3 O'CLOCK
GINGER HUSTON
315 LAKE COURT
COME IN COSTUME
PLEASE REPLY

GOVERNOR'S TRADE

As the West was being populated, Ginger explained, everyone had his own trade, but the governor spent a good share of his time signing papers. She asked the guests to stand in a straight line and in turn requested each one to choose a trade to follow, and to show how it was done. At a signal the housewife began to scrub, the carpenter to hammer, the woodsman to chop trees, and the governor to sign papers. Then Ginger gave the governor the privilege of assuming any other trade when he wished. As long as the governor signed papers, the others followed their own professions. But as soon as the governor changed to another trade, everyone else had to do as he was doing.

The first governor chose to sign his papers for only a few seconds, and suddenly began to spade with the farmers. The butchers, bakers, and doctors soon began to spade; but the poor little housewife kept right on scrubbing. She had to drop out of the game. The next round the governor caught four offenders. Soon only one tradesman was left. He became the governor. The game was played three times before Ginger stopped it and asked the governor to become an ordinary frontiersman and the other guests to be Indians.

WAR CRIES

"A smart frontiersman," Ginger explained, "had to know whether Indians were hostile or friendly, and some of them could tell by the war cries." She blindfolded the frontiersman and asked him to go to an Indian, who was to let out three dreadful war cries. The frontiersman knew the voice, and so the Indian proved himself friendly and became the frontiersman. Since the second frontiersman could not identify the first Indian he approached, he called him hostile and went to another Indian whose voice he did know. The third frontiersman could not guess the three Indians who let out cries for him; so he chose an Indian at random to take his place. One time a frontiersman guessed the voice of a boy who had been in the center of the circle, so he asked another lad to take his place.

When all the Westerners were familiar with the cries of Indians—that is, when everyone had a chance to be in the center of the circle—Ginger suggested that they all do their part in aiding the pony express. She divided the guest into relay teams and gave each leader a letter. At a signal the team members passed the letters down the lines until they reached the last men. These quickly ran to the front of the lines and passed the letters down. The race continued until one team had its leader again at the head.

Ginger then suggested that at times the pony express had to deliver the mail under difficulties. She asked the team members to pass the letters between their legs. For the third race, they passed them over their heads.

STAKING CLAIM

Ginger opened one letter. "Shucks," she said. "This note was supposed to tell me where my claim is located. There are lots of words in the note which are all mixed up. If I give you each a list of them, will you help me figure them out?"

She gave each guest a slip of paper on which were twisted landmarks, reading: "lavley, lihl, remast, rete, reriv, saps, nibac, slafl, dipars, putms." After working for several minutes, a boy gave Ginger a paper reading: "valley, hill, stream, tree, river, pass, cabin, falls, rapids, stump."

"Thanks for helping me out," said the hostess. "If you ever happen to be around these parts after I build my cabin, I'd like to have you stay with me and my family. But I want to make sure that you know how to blow out candles; so if you stay up later than I do, you won't have trouble."

CANDLE BLOWING

Ginger placed a thick candle on the table and lighted it. In turn she blindfolded each guest, turned him around three times, asked him to take three steps backward, three steps forward, and then without bending over to blow out the candle with one puff. It sounded so easy that several of the boys laughed at the idea, for there was the candle right in front of the starting point. But they soon learned that for some reason or other it wasn't so easy to take just the same size steps both ways, and then blow their one big puff in just the correct direction. In fact, only one child, a little girl, blew out the taper.

"Well, never mind," said Ginger. "We'll want to sit around the campfire when you come and sing songs, anyway. Let's try a few now." Her mother played the piano as the boys and girls crooned out some of the tunes they knew.

REFRESHMENTS

In the meantime, Ginger set up tables and put red and white checked paper spreads over them, centering each one with a big round white candle. When the songfest was over, she served her guests scalloped corn with bacon, hot rolls, hot chocolate, and ice cream.

SUGGESTIONS

Children from ten to fourteen years of age may give this party. As there are no running games, it may be given in almost any room. Church and school groups may give the party if the leaders divide the guests into groups of not more than twelve children for the candle blowing contest and the "governor's trade."

If there is time, the guests might put on a home talent show, speaking pieces and singing songs as the characters whom they represent might present them. An "Indian hunt" as outlined in the Daniel Boone Party (page 122), or a "shooting" contest as in the Indian Party (page 103), would be appropriate for this party.

MATERIALS NEEDED

Invitations: Paper, pencil or pen and India ink, crayons or water colors.
Decorations: Red and white checked tablecloths, candles.
Games: Pencil and paper for each guest, blindfold, letter for each relay team, candle, lists of names of landmarks with letters twisted.

CHRISTMAS
PARTY

DECEMBER 21,
3 O'CLOCK

JACK HOLT

866 BARNES
AVE

Christmas Party

THE SOUND OF "JINGLE BELLS, JINGLE BELLS" RANG THROUGH the air as Jack Holt sent his little paper Santa Clauses through the mail to invite children to his Christmas party. Over each Santa's shoulder was slung a bag filled with wonderful surprises, little paper toys which could be pulled out of slits in the picture. On each toy was written part of the invitation.

By cutting pine boughs and placing them over the mantel and around the archways of the front room of his home, Jack created a scene which resembled a spot in a northern forest where Santa might have one of his workshops. As a finishing touch, he hung a great Christmas wreath in the doorway.

Just before the party, Jack brought two small untrimmed trees into the living room and then hid all manner of trimmings, strings of cranberries, tinsel, shiny balls, small angels, and ornaments which he had made himself by cutting small figures out of pictures in magazines, mounting them on construction paper, and putting strings through little holes in the top.

DECORATING TREES

As the guests arrived, Jack gave them little stockings, some cut of blue construction paper and some of red. He explained that those holding red stockings would join in decorating the tree on one side of the room and those with blue stockings would join in decorating the other. He ruled that a child should hang a trimming on the tree before he searched for another. The tots began to scamper about looking all over for the brightly colored ornaments. With shrieks of laughter each one fastened his trimming just where he wanted it to go, until at last the two trees were as beautifully decorated as any seen anywhere—or at least the children declared they were.

153

"Now we are all ready for Santa here," said Jack, "but I have just had word that he is having trouble harnessing his reindeer. Mother, you tell them how to play Santa and the reindeer."

"Of course you all know how bright the snow is," said his mother. "Now just pretend there was snow almost everywhere and you had to look for a reindeer. It would almost make you blind, wouldn't it? That is why we are going to blindfold Santa for this game, and we'll give his reindeer a bell to aid the old man in the search."

She selected two children to play the parts and instructed the others to form a circle around them. According to her directions the two characters moved without running within the circle. Santa kept calling, "Blitzen! Blitzen!" after which the reindeer rang his bell. Somehow or other the pet seemed to evade the old man every time he came close to him, but at last he was caught. Each character chose a successor, but the new Santa searched for "Donner." One by one the reindeer were caught.

PACKING SANTA'S BAG

"Now let's help Santa pack his bag," said Jack. The children sat in a circle, and one began the game by saying, "I helped Santa pack his bag, and in it I put an apple." His choice of an article started with "A." The next person said, "I helped Santa pack his bag, and in it I put an apple and a baby doll." Each child in turn repeated the long list of things in the old fellow's bag and added a new article whose first letter began with the next letter in the alphabet. Soon a little boy forgot one of the toys; so he dropped out of the game, only listening to his pals. One by one the other guests made mistakes until only one little girl was left playing. She was given a picture book as a prize.

COMING DOWN THE CHIMNEY

"It's about time for Santa to start coming down the chimney," said the young host as he covered a table with some newspapers and placed in its center a home-drawn picture of a house with a big chimney. The game was played like "pin the tail on the donkey," only each guest was given a Santa Claus seal which he was directed to paste on top of the chimney in the picture. Jack blindfolded each guest in turn, turned him around three times, wet his sticker with a damp cloth, and let him walk to the table. When the picture was finished it was really very pretty, with Santa's climbing everywhere.

SINGING CAROLS

"Santa loves to hear boys and girls singing Christmas carols," said Jack. "Let's gather around the piano and sing some that we all know best."

They sang all the songs in a tiny book and would have kept right on warbling had Jack not looked at the clock. It was half past five. "I guess it is time for some gifts," said the host and passed out a toy of construction paper to each guest. Before very long, the boys and girls discovered that there were two of each kind. Then Jack told them that they could find their partners for the grand march to supper by pairing them. The two holders of horns were soon side by side; then the drum holders came together; and before long each guest had a partner.

REFRESHMENTS

Round and round the room the guests marched, following their host and his partner, until at last they entered the dining room. In the center of the table was a great mound of popcorn with a Santa driving his reindeer on top. At each place stood a funny little soldier with marshmallow body, tinfoil wrapped chocolate bud head, and gumdrop legs and arms. The various parts of his body were held together with toothpicks, and another toothpick at the back helped him to stand.

Creamed chipped beef and peas were served in patty shells. There was also a quantity of steaming hot chocolate with marshmallows bobbing up and down in each cup, little Santa Claus cookie men with tiny candies in their packs, and ice cream fashioned in Christmas wreaths.

Children from eight to ten years of age will enjoy this party. If popcorn stringing is substituted for the alphabetical packing of Santa's pack, children as young as five years of age may give it. Church and school classes may give the party by dividing the children into small groups of between ten and twelve.

POPCORN STRINGING

For a popcorn stringing contest, give each child a long stout thread and a large darning needle. Place popped corn where all may reach it, or give each child a little bowl of it. At a signal, instruct the children to start stringing. Each child may hang his string on the tree which he helped to decorate. Cranberries may be substituted for popped corn.

"Toyshop" as described in the Doll Party (page 142) would also fit into these plans as a substitute.

MATERIALS NEEDED

Invitations: Paper, pencil, paints or crayons, scissors.

Decorations: Pine boughs, wreaths, popcorn, Santa and reindeer, candy soldiers made of marshmallows, toothpicks, chocolate buds, and gumdrops.

Games: Untrimmed Christmas trees, ornaments including those made of magazine pictures mounted on construction paper, blue and red stockings of construction paper, handkerchief for blindfolding, bell, newspapers, picture of house with chimney, Santa Claus seals, damp cloth, book of carols, pairs of construction paper toys.

Favors: Picture book.

156

Index

CLASSIFIED INDEX OF GAMES

ACTIVE GAMES

HANDWORK

HUNTS

MIXERS

MUSICAL GAMES

OUTDOOR GAMES

PRACTICAL JOKES

159

QUIET GAMES

SKILL GAMES

TEAM GAMES

WRITING GAMES